Is Home Your Happy Place?

Christy Diane Farr

Cover artwork from zenbitsart.com

Cover design by Niki Lenhart
nikilen-designs.com

Published by Paper Angel Press

paperangelpress.com

ISBN 978-1-944412-63-0 (Trade Paperback)

10 9 8 7 6 5 4 3 2

FIRST EDITION

Learn more at
The Unruly Woman
theunrulywoman.com

To Seth, Kira Liberty, and The Beautiful One
for filling our happy place with more love, laughter,
and support than I imagined possible

Table of Contents

Acknowledgements

I googled "how to write book acknowledgements" and, aside from the controversial *e*, it sounds pretty straightforward. I'm supposed to name every single person who contributed to my knowledge, supported me, or inspired me to write this book. If that's true, *oh please let it not be true,* show me to the special library where we keep all of the books written about the people who made possible all of the books that I've loved.

This is my first book and every step of the way, I had no idea how to do what needed to be done. Several people tried to help me write this book. The general consensus was that my grasp on grammar is mostly just by the ends of my fingertips, so I need to thank Laureen Hudson for editing. And you did the thing nobody else could or would. You told me what order to put the chapters in, shoving me off a cliff I'd been looking over for three years. Also, thank you for the pep talks, taunting, guidance, and seemingly endless support of my heart's work. You've been trying to get this thing published for years and I'm grateful you never gave up.

That brings me to Steven Radecki. You are my web guru, publisher dude, and official gatekeeper of the legitimacy of my dream. Lots of people think this work is important, but you showed me how to make it a real business. And, for the love of all things glittery, thank you for remembering that I said, "Well, you know how much I love an Unruly Woman." The name and the vision you've helped me craft for all of this is simply flawless.

And there are the 1200+ Unrulies who've accompanied me on this space healing journey so far. Because you were brave enough to share your heartbreaks, challenges, and dreams, I was able to hear and share all of what follows and the work that continues from today on. I humbly thank you. Your courage healed and inspired me. Specifically, let me thank those who said yes to that very first workshop, the 7 "founders" who refused to let me stop when it ended, and the real rockstars who keep coming back until they take back their lives. To those who've helped spread the word — relentlessly harassing neighbors, loved ones, coworkers, and even strangers to try space healing — I extend to you my deepest bow of gratitude. Without you, no one would have ever known about any of this.

Thank you Oriah Mountain Dreamer for shattering me with your words and inspiring me with your way of being in the world. So much of what's magical about my life today is because of you and "The Invitation" you've gifted us all. Anne Lamott, although you don't know me from Eve, thank you for writing the way that I think. Reading your books made me believe this was possible and your mastery inspires me to up my game every day.

To my parents who have been worrying about/supporting me for many, many moons and loving me hard, thank you. To my friends who still love me even though I've mostly sucked at friendship, thank you. Tisha Morris, thank you for blazing the "passionate but relatively unknown woman writes a book" trail. Your book planted the seed that blossomed into mine.

Seth and Kira Liberty, you two gave me purpose when I believed I had none. To my amazement and deep joy, you've encouraged me as I stumbled through figuring out who I am and how to be it. Every single thing I am today is because you chose me, including my wisdom hairs. I love the people you've become. Jake and Joey you have a forever place in my heart.

And to The Beautiful One, Dyani Heinz, you're asleep with your arm around me right now. Your love wrecks me in all of the best ways. Thank you for waiting for me, even though you didn't know it was me you were waiting for. Thank you for saying "yes" the day we figured it out, and for continuing to say yes to me every day since then. Thank you for working oh so hard, mothering brilliantly, and teaching me all of these really important things I (somehow) made it to 40 without knowing. Thank you for being my equal. Thank you for not needing this book… and for reading it anyway.

I can barely see the words on my laptop screen for the tears of gratitude flooding my eyes and pouring down my cheeks. I'm overwhelmed by the love and support I've received from all of you (and many others) in the nearly eight years since I started the business that became The Unruly Woman. Having a dream job for your day job is a gift far too few of us have opened and I'm grateful every day to do my work in the world. I promise to continue to do my part to make more.

Thank you. Thank you. Thank you.

Warning:
I Am Not Like The Others

"I may have had a negative reaction to some of the previous clutter-related articles. Now I get it. The author is writing from the perspective of someone who helps hoarders or shopaholics. And I found balance ages ago so I don't get it. But ultimately the question is who gets to decide what is or is not clutter? Or what is an acceptable level of stuff? How about an article that helps people determine for themselves what may be signals that they have a problem rather than advising everyone to just get rid of possessions for the sake of getting rid of them?"

While I think those are valid questions, I was more than a little surprised to read that someone who'd been reading the series of articles which were the foundation for this book didn't already know the answers. First of all, it is not my intention to separate everyone from everything they own. I mean, really? Who wants that job, even in this economy?

You may have already recognized that I am not everyone's taste. If not, and before you go any further, allow me to tell you how I roll. I tell stories, sometimes painfully long ones, in a world where I'm encouraged to be brief, redundant, and organized by bullets because you are supposedly busy, bored, and overwhelmed by people like me offering information about how to change your life. If I've ever had a "clickable" title on one of my articles it was an accident. I refuse to promote gratitude during November or fresh starts in January. I will not invite you to something useful and free just to follow up with an invitation to the thing you really need at a cost that I've dramatically inflated simply because "they" say that you'll think it's high quality.

I will not pretend I am something I'm not just so you'll feel reassured about my professionalism, nor will I tell you that you need to hire me, come to one of my workshops, or read my articles. (Yes, I'm aware that by many people's standards, this means I suck at marketing. I'm okay with that... stay with me here.)

I trust you.

I trust you to know if your needs are in alignment with my work.

If I write something that resonates for you, I trust you'll read it (again and again, if that's what it takes). I trust that if you like what I've written that you'll "Like" it and if you think people in your life would enjoy it, I trust you to share it with them. I trust you to get what you want and ask for what you need. I trust that you'll hire me if you want to work with me.

It is my intention to use whatever is within my means to support the loving transformation of the world. People are suffering, sometimes too stuck in the suffering to make the desired change, and my life's work is about cultivating freedom.

What's "within my means" includes 10 years as a professional organizer, plus seven and counting as the life coach who became The Unruly Woman. I have some random but powerful skills and abilities — coaching, teaching, writing. I am passionate about women, creative people, children, our planet, equality, non-violent solutions to conflict with others and ourselves, and living simply. It is my love of those people and things that keep me doing this day after day.

These are all I have to work with, all I can use to do my part to heal the world.

In the summer of 2011, I was struggling, confused about my work, and I asked for direction from the Powers That Be. I asked what I could do with my business — the coaching, writing, and teaching — to really make a difference in people's lives. I want that… I think we all do. The answer was breath-taking.

Prepare them to travel lightly through what lies ahead by releasing attachments to things and old wounds.

I not so metaphorically cried back, "Oh no, not that… anything but that! I don't know how to do that! One woman thinks the fat is her problem, while another thinks her husband is the problem, and yet another blames work. I don't know how to create something that works for all of these people." There was some banging of heads against walls, shaking of fists at the sky, tears of frustration and more than a little fear.

Then, I found this, in *Feng Shui Your Life: The Quick Guide to Decluttering Your Home and Renewing Your Life,* by Tisha Morris:

"Our home is simply a mirror of our self. A common example of this is how, when the home is messy and in disarray, we may feel mentally disheveled as well. The better your home feels, the better you will feel. And when you feel better — physically, neatly, or emotionally — then life will simply flow better for you. This is the beauty and magic of feng shui. The positive changes you make in your home will be reflected out into your life."

(Cue full circle moment music.)

Your house reflects your inner state and you can either break that pattern by changing your inner state, which allows the conditions in your house to change, or you can change the conditions in your house. It doesn't matter which side you tend first.

Once that lock is broken, the changes that you want to make in all of the other areas of life become possible.

Are you stuck? Are you sick of it? Do you believe that releasing that which no longer serves you from your physical environment will free you to make the changes you desire? And if not, are you willing to suspend that disbelief for a day, a week, or a month to try a different approach to change?

Yes. Yes. Yes. It only takes three yeses to change your life. Basically, I'm an experienced guide who's looking for people who are ready to take a transformative space healing journey. If you're not stuck, I'm not for you. If you're stuck but you're not yet sick of it, I'm still not for you. And the same goes for the last ones, if you don't believe or can't suspend the disbelief, then what I'm proposing can't possibly be the support you need. The good news is, my way is not the only way.

So, who gets to decide what is or is not clutter? That would be you. It doesn't matter if you're a client, a student in one of my space healing workshops (or another teacher's method for that matter), or person who found this book on a park bench... these are your decisions to make.

If you're not stuck, I celebrate with you! If you are stuck but you're not ready to release certain things, I don't care. We can work on the rest of it. Either way, I trust you to make decisions about your stuff.

I know how to ask the right questions, broach specific emotional areas, and equip you with the ability to find your answers. After four years of sharing the ideas and methods that follow, I know that what most people need is new information and inspiration, tools for digging into the old energies, encouragement, and accountability. I've done my best to include as much of that in this book as possible, but the control is yours. I suppose that's the good news and the bad, right?

Being out of control of our lives is what gets us stuck to begin with.

What is an acceptable level of stuff? Everyone has a different definition here. For me, it's about living within my means — physically, mentally, emotionally, spiritually, and of course, financially. As for "an article that helps people determine for themselves what may be signals that they have a problem rather than advising everyone to just get rid of possessions for the sake of getting rid of them"… well, you can figure that out for yourself when you get to 'Is Your Clutter Clinical?'.

So, there you have it. You've been warned. I'm not like the others. This approach is not like the others. And if you still want to proceed, then it means you too are not like the others and we'll work just fine together.

Welcome to the adventure ~

Six Kinds of Stuff That's Keeping You Stuck

When people come to my workshops, they are ready to make a big change. They aren't looking for the "just right" organizing system, or to buy a planner that will magically restore their sanity. (Not that they hate those ideas, they've just tried them all before, and those things didn't solve the problem.) They are stuck, and they are sick of it; and they know it's going to take action to make right what has gone wrong in their worlds.

I tell them all the time that space healing is about manipulating ourselves into making decisions and taking action. My job, of course, is to make the decision-making possible and taking action not suck. It's a supportive, party-like atmosphere, complete with fresh, new ways to consider our relationship with stuff.

We look for things that no longer serve us, ways to let go that will make space for what we really want in our lives. In the spirit of strong starts, here are six types of things that you can release right now to shake up your space!

1. *Stuff that makes you feel crazy.* Food storage containers, for the love of all things glittery, are a great example of crazy-making stuff that must be tamed. They're square and round, deep and shallow, ripple- and flat-bottomed, and possess a nearly complete absence of stack-ability. The madness of trying to manage them far outweighs anything even remotely resembling the convenience that would be using them *if only* we could actually find their matching lids. All but what is truly manageable must go… in peace, of course.

2. *Stuff that's broken.* If you're not going to fix it, let it go. It's either worth the time, money, and energy it takes to make it work, or it just isn't. Free it, and free yourself.

3. *Stuff that makes you hang onto an unpleasant past.* A hundred years ago, when I was separating the material evidence of my first marriage into his and hers, I took the children's movies (as I was going to be the one with the children), my few romantic comedies, and all of the Will Smith and John Travolta movies (a marital-dissolution rebellion that, in hindsight, seems rather lame). They sat on the top shelf of a bookcase in that breathtakingly yellow bedroom at my mom's house, alongside the rest of my worldly possessions. Every day, as I walked back and forth tending my babies and trying to figure out what in the hell I was going to do with my life now, I thought, *"Those are the movies I got in the divorce."* Finally, after a couple of months, I realized that having that thought a few dozen times every day was probably not helping me. I gave them back and moved on.

4. *Stuff that's expired.* In my workshops, the expiration date purge is one of the most fun challenges. It's surprising how easily expired medicines and food can build up. Take a look in your bathroom cabinet, refrigerator, and pantry. I bet you'll be surprised how

much is in there that you're not even seeing anymore. (If you have food that you're not going to use that isn't yet expired, go ahead and donate it to the food bank before it's too late!)

5. *Stuff that sucks.* Look for everything else you have around that just isn't showing up in the world the way you want or need it to. "Goodbye, cleaning supplies that don't clean! Out with the hair products that make my hair do the opposite of what I want! See you later, yarn that I purchased before I found out that yarn can feel oh-so-much better than you feel! And to those pants that actually do make my butt look bigger than it is. It's time for all of you to move along!"

6. *Stuff that used to be a good idea.* This might be the supplies for the craft project for which you have lost the thrill, or exercise equipment you just had to have but don't actually use. It could be that charming little shoot of bamboo that the cats can't bear to let grow, or that slinky little dress you bought after the last breakup that simply isn't suitable for public appearances.

This short list is a playful insight into a technique I use repeatedly throughout this book that I affectionately refer to as "mind games."

New ways of being require new ways of thinking. It's my job to creep into your mind and cast doubt, challenge, and even boldly rebel against your old, tired thoughts, beliefs, and patterns. (My clients call that The Little Christy In My Head.) Don't worry. I'm not coming for all your thoughts, just the ones that are standing between you and your true self.

If the way you thought about your stuff up until this moment crafted the reality that caused you to pick up this book, then it's time for mind games. You'll see that the idea behind the expiration date challenge can be applied to all aspects of your life. Since my kids are going to college soon, my maternity clothes are expired. Books I've read and have no intention of reading again are expired. Even those hair bangs that birds could nest in expired in 1990, so I let them go. If our relationship with this stuff was intended to be eternal, caskets would be bigger. Once something expires, we can let it go.

Mind games help us revisit our relationships with everything around us.

How to Use This Book

When I had the big epiphany about healing ourselves from the outside in, my first attempt to share it was called Sick of Being Stuck September. I invited all 143 people on my newsletter list, and the readers from a blogging gig I had back in the day. It lasted 27 days and included daily action challenges, a dozen group calls, a virtual place to connect with one another, and my undivided attention to process the sticky stuff. It was free and just over 600 people said yes. It was a truly extraordinary experience.

In the four years since then, I've been offering introductory space healing workshops and a master class for graduates, plus working with clients one-on-one. My approach has been refined with each new season, deepening my understanding of what's possible. Sick of Being Stuck morphed into Clean Slate and that became Tame Your Space. This book is the next evolution.

It's my intention to include the best of all four years on these pages, to take what's working here in my community and make it accessible to everyone else who feels like the other resources aren't cutting it. This book is a love offering — not just from me but from every single person with whom I've collaborated until now — to you. I want most for you to feel supported enough to move forward on this space healing journey because it's a vital part of your personal evolution. And the world is waiting for you to be the one you came to this planet to be.

In addition to the mind games I mentioned above, you'll find oodles of stories. They are my stories and the stories of the brave souls who came before you. Some stories are funny and others heart-breaking, and they are all a window into the space healing process. Take the information and inspiration that resonates for you and release the rest.

Also, you'll find bits and pieces of what I reluctantly call "my method." I say reluctantly because there are a great many experts in the self-help industry who have big, fancy, detailed, well-documented methods. They have graphics and trademarked titles and certified training programs so the expertness can be spread throughout the world by those who can afford the training.

To be clear, I'm not knocking those experts or their programs. I'm a fan of dreams coming to life and I applaud anyone who is living and sharing their dream in that way.

I'm just not that girl.

I have a method. It's simple and it works if you work it.

Here it is:

1. Release what no longer serves you.

2. Organize what remains.

3. Clean.

Most of my time is spent blowing up people's beliefs about themselves and their stuff enough to get them to start with step one. We are exposing the old wounds that set these patterns into motion, so they can be healed. Once you tend the energetic source of these unproductive patterns, it becomes possible to work basically any method, and mine will suffice for those who don't have one they already subscribe to.

I'm sure you already gathered that of the three steps, "Release what no longer serves you" is where all of the radical transformation becomes possible. During space healing workshops, I use daily action challenges to get people releasing again. In the beginning, they include very detailed action with a specific room or zone and a certain number of items to release: "Go to your bedroom closet. Find 27 things that no longer serve you and release them."

As we continue, the challenges shift from specific zones in the home to certain types of clutter. (Find 27 pieces of paper that no longer serve you and release them.) Unless we are talking about one great big action for the day, I always use the same number for action challenges. I've been teasing people with that number for years and I'm finally going to write down why it's always 27 with me.

In preparation for that first Sick of Being Stuck workshop, I reached out to Tisha Morris, the author of the Feng Shui book that inspired my epiphany. I was mindlessly flipping through her book while I outlined my plan — the support calls, group dynamics, and the daily challenges based on this quote which was the inspiration for her book.

If you want to change your life, move 27 things in your home.

> *- Chinese proverb*

If moving 27 things in your home could change lives back in the day, what kind of change could we cultivate in our overwhelmed modern spaces by releasing 27 things? Was it enough to release 27 things every single day until we once again felt free to live passionate, purposeful lives?

Once I started using the number, I heard all sorts of stories from clients about other ways the number resonated for them. Doreen Virtues' Angel Numbers 101 says of the number 27, "Congratulations! Your optimism is attracting wonderful situations and relationships. Stay positive, as this attitude is working in your favor." It turns out, there are even 27 bones in the human hand. How about we celebrate by using our hands to take action to reclaim our lives?

Most importantly, I realized that it was a number that was not so small that people dismissed it but also it was not so big that people were overwhelmed by being given the challenge to find and release items that no longer served them. People are more agreeable with 27 than they are with any other number I've tried to use!

When I first started writing this book, I could only imagine it as a workshop in print. I had the chapters labeled as day 1, day 2, and so on, and each chapter included a daily action challenge, plus a mind game to challenge the way you see your stuff. But I knew that the remarkable workshop success was less about my "method" and more about the collaboration each client had with me and their classmates — the group calls, Facebook group conversations, and private sessions. These are the sacred containers where it feels safe to share pictures, confess paralyzing secrets, dig into the stories behind stuck energy patterns, and release old wounds. This is where the healing happens, the healing that makes a new way of being become possible.

To be honest, I nearly lost my mind trying to put together a print version of the workshop without the human interaction. I found it entirely pointless, frankly, as though I'd be adding one more empty promise to the bottomless pit of self-help resources in which all of my clients had already nearly drowned. I couldn't bear it.

Instead I poured myself into the workshops and individual sessions for the last four years. The beautiful work we all did together took that initial workshop-in-a-book idea, a tiny seed that looked utterly useless but held so much potential, and allowed it to blossom into the life-changing invitation you are holding in your hands right now.

It's not a workshop in a book but it has the best of the best of what I teach in a space healing workshop. It's not an elaborate system but it does have a simple, powerful method to get you moving again. It's not a step by step "how to" guide for making a specific kind of home (zen, welcoming, pretty, or whatever else you've heard your home "should" be) but it will guide you as you figure out a vision that's true for you and move into alignment with it.

Your physical environment is a reflection of your inner world. If there's a gap between reality and the way you want your home to look, feel, and function, then I want to help you close that gap. This book contains everything I know about how to close that gap, delivered the only way I know how. It's a conversation about space healing. Dig in one chapter at a time. I've included some examples of the action challenges from my workshops where it makes sense to give you ideas about how to apply what you've read to your space. But don't get all strung out about them. Use them if they are useful. If you can't bear to, keep reading. You'll learn how to heal your space by reading the stories. The challenges will be here when you're ready to take action.

Your space healing journey has a specific but un-named number of steps. To complete the processing of the backlog that's overwhelming you, it's going to take a certain amount of action. Obviously, the more you do, the faster your journey will go. Whether it's 10, 100, or 1000 hours you have ahead of you, now is the perfect time to begin (or begin again if you already journeyed a bit before wandering off). If you can give it an hour a week, then it will take a certain amount of time. If you can give yourself two hours a week, you'll be done in half that time. If you can give four hours most weeks, you'll reach your destination in one-quarter of the time.

Your commitment to this space healing journey is real. Any progress counts. More progress will cultivate more change. Even if you wander off, keep coming back. I'll always be sitting here waiting to pick up where we left off. I believe in this process. It's changed my life. No matter how long it takes to journey back to the truth of who you are, know that you deserve to invest every single bit of time, energy, money, and support it takes to get you home. You are worth it.

Yes, I'm sure.

The Heart of Space Healing: Releasing Stories

It feels important to start by sharing my own "letting go" stories about the deep personal evolution I've experienced throughout the four years I've been offering this workshop.

I've been digging into the depths of my memory to find particularly intimate, powerful, or even painful stories. And I just realized that the fact that I'm having a hard time recalling them actually tells far more about the power of this process than the stories would.

I released what no longer served me.

When I let go of that stuff I let go of the stories they represented.

Years ago, The Voices In My Head (TVIMH) showed me an image of people toting around trunks filled with souvenirs representing old untended fears, heartbreaks, and other unresolved matters of the heart. Some of us drag them behind us, others strap them on our backs, and still others search for emotionally over-competent (read: codependent) people to manage them for us.

The work that I do with my clients is about unpacking their trunks and, of course, I have my own to unpack. I've done a great many things to unload the emotional baggage that was weighing me down when I started this journey — writing, studying, dancing, therapy, coaching, energy healing, bodywork.

And because I wholeheartedly believe that the state of my inner world is reflected in my physical space — Yes, I said that my emotional and mental well-being are reflected in my home — tending to my physical space was vital to that healing journey. I had to practice what I was preaching to my clients.

I had to release what no longer served me.

I did it. I've been doing it for four years and I will continue to do it as I evolve into newer, truer versions of myself. I do it because I know my space can hold me where I no longer want to be or my space can be the kind of environment that pulls me forward, home to the truth of who I am.

Does that mean I don't have any more space healing stories of my own to tell? No, I've found a few to share with you. But they may not be as sexy as I'd hoped they would be. I released the stuff that no longer serves me and the pain and heat and heartbreak are gone, too. My space is simple and powerful and full of truth… and my heart is finally free.

Releasing Codependency

My daughter recently became upset when I released a sweater to which she believed I still had an attachment. This did not come, as one might assume, from her projecting her beliefs about keeping stuff upon me or that she'd given it to me as a gift or that she wanted it for herself. No, those reasons would have been much easier for me to face. Her alarm was about something deeper, something that hurt my heart a bit.

For the last several years, my daughter watched me release and release and release to try to make space in myself in a home where there was far too much stuff. I was sincerely overwhelmed by the possessions that felt (at least to me) as though they exceeded the capacity of the space we had to contain them. And while my daughter and I were prepared to live more simply, the other two family members were not. So I did all that I knew to do to cultivate sanity for myself.

Every time I felt like I was going to go mad, I got rid of more of my stuff.

In this moment of reflection, I can see how this was alarming to my daughter. I would go into my super-stuffed shared closet and come out with three bags of only my things to donate. The books piled up around the bookcase would suddenly have space to be shelved and two boxes of my books would be taken to the used book store. Each trip to the donation center had us dropping off mostly things that had belonged to my daughter and me.

I did not realize that she even noticed how clutter-clearing went down at our house.

And I damn sure did not realize that she'd archived it as me sacrificing my stuff because other people wouldn't do their part.

At first, I cringed that this was not what I wanted her to learn about maneuvering relationships but you know what? Maybe it's perfect.

I took back my inner world one external thing at a time.

I released furniture, household decorations, art, pictures, clothing, books, linens, recreational equipment, and more paper than you can imagine. No corner of our two-bedroom condominium remained untouched during this period of time. It didn't happen all at once but every time I taught another round of this workshop my belongings shrank more and more into something that honestly represented who I was. As each new layer was released, I began to feel more free.

I don't miss any of that stuff.

Through four years of intense clutter-clearing, there were only two things I later wished I had back. One came back to me for free and the other I replaced for $30. I understand the temptation to keep everything just in case you need it someday. I'd been living that way. But the truth was that I felt too crowded and too overwhelmed to live each day I was actually experiencing because of the chaos in my physical space. I was sacrificing joy, peace, creativity, and sanity on any given day because I was unwilling to let go of the past and the future.

I was always in choice. Always.

When I couldn't control what they did with their stuff, I focused on my relationship with my stuff. When I felt frustrated about the stacks of clothes that others wouldn't or couldn't wear cluttering up the closet, I found everything that I couldn't or wouldn't wear and let it go. When their art supplies and instruments sat unused, I turned my attention to my own neglected creative debris. When the stuff piled up around the opposite side of the bed made me want to scream, I turned my attention to making my side of the bed as simple and clean as possible.

Was it the same as them tending their stuff? No, of course not. But since I started teaching this workshop, I took back my life by releasing everything that no longer served me.

Eventually, I ended that relationship. There were many, many factors that led me to realize that was what felt true for me but this piece was one of the most empowering experiences of my life. I know that I couldn't have cultivated this truth without dealing with myself and my stuff in this way.

Yes, this is decidedly what I want my daughter to know about the way "stuff" and life intersect. I **want her to know that no matter what relation-ship or situation she finds herself in, no matter how far away from her truth she finds herself, she can make it back.** She needs to be willing to face the truth of her situation. She must tend her business. She can let go of whatever is keeping her stuck. The journey begins not by obsessing over everyone else but by facing the woman in the mirror.

Releasing Clothes

Letting go of my fat clothes was hard.

I felt afraid.

What if I gained back what I lost? What if I failed? What if I couldn't keep the promise that I made to myself?

Oh my goodness! Seriously? Was I actually willing to be afraid that I was so out of alignment that I would allow myself to sit (as in be idle) and eat (read: overeat) my way to nakedness? No way! I am no longer that woman.

In one visit to the closet, I released every single thing that was too big for me. Since that day, I've released everything else that became too big as I make my way back to my true body.

On the flip side, I also had clothes that were too small. Releasing the dreamy Skinny Christy Myth took far more work. No . . . courage. No . . . healing. Yes, it took far more healing. It took three years of trips to that closet to let go of all of the clothes that belonged to the thin woman I once was.

Have I released the idea that I will once again be that size? Absolutely not. But I've released the woman I used to be. I've released the idea that who I am today is somehow unworthy of being embraced, celebrated, accepted . . . loved by me and those around me.

I realized that I am on my way to something new with this body. I'm loving it more than ever. I'm moving and actually *using* this body in ways that I never dared to before. I'm eating in a way that honors this body. The calories burned and taken in (plus whatever other factors are at play at this exact moment in my personal evolution) cultivated this ever-changing, curvy, strong 3-D awesomeness and I'm no longer willing to will my body to be anything but what it is.

This letting go took time. I went into that closet again and again searching for that which no longer served me. The first layer was all that I wouldn't wear even if I was that size. Yes, much to my surprise, I owned and was storing clothes that were too worn or didn't work for me because of the shape or color or style.

The next time I went searching, I found others that survived the first cut but suddenly seemed like they were taking up space. The next time, having lost a little more weight, I started trying on everything. If it wasn't something that I thought I could reasonably get into in the next season or so, I let it go.

This release session was quite intense for me. I had to slide my "favorite" jeans just past my knees, be with the reality of that being as far as they would go, and then *choose* to accept that it would take an act of congress to get me back into them.

I made the choice to let go.

I did this, in part, with the realization that if I was ever that size again, I'd have the most amazing time buying myself a new pair of favorite jeans.

During that space healing session, I saved back one paper box of clothes that I truly loved and would want to have when I got back to that size. I integrated into my closet what finally fit and I released the rest.

Every single thing in my closet fits my body . . . the body I love and have a beautiful relationship with TODAY.

Releasing People

Letting go of stuff can be hard.

Letting go of people makes releasing stuff feel like child's play.

In addition to the oodles of physical clutter I've been writing about releasing I've let go of a lot of people throughout this journey. Now, don't get me wrong. I didn't line up everyone I know so I could vote a bunch of them off the island that is my life. That's not what I'm talking about.

Okay, maybe that island thing did happen a time or two but I reserve that dramatic action for very specific situations where I feel that a relationship with someone is no longer true for me and the other person loses their ever-loving mind and brings mental, emotional, or physical violence into my life. *Be nice or leave* is a powerful guideline to help with this sort of decision making.

I can now see that most of the people releases are about letting go of my expectations of others, giving them the love and space to be themselves, and asking them to do the same for me.

I finally stopped expecting my children's father to show up in the ways that I thought mattered. Instead, I gave him the space to show up in their lives however it felt true for him. I stepped out of the circle between him and the children and allowed him to be in action with them (instead of reaction to me). He also gets the blessed opportunity to experience the natural consequences of his actions instead of me thrusting myself into the middle and manipulating outcomes.

I released my friends from any expectations I had about how they should be with me. Instead, I invited them to be as connected to me as felt true for them given the *natural* ebb and flow of life. As time passes, our interests, energy, availability, proximity, and dozens of other factors shape how we show up in the world. The passing of time is doing the exact same thing for the people around us. Instead of clinging desperately to the way my friendships used to be, I let go and allowed them to grow and change with me. This helps everyone involved release the guilt, celebrate the love that lives between us, and deeply enjoy the times when togetherness is true for us.

I've released my children from the expectations that they become any of the millions of things I thought they "should" or would be. I will continue to do it every single time I feel the squeeze of their truth being pressed against my expectations. This one is so hard. Also, releasing them to live their truth is one of the most important pieces of this work I will do.

I've released what feels like an endless line of expectations I discovered that I had of people in my community about my business. I expected them to do a great many things that would have resulted in the successful execution of my business plan — hire me, refer others, keep promises, like my ideas, reach out for support, etc.

(That is a short sample of the expectations and yes, it feels ridiculous now that I'm typing it all out. Still, it's true that I felt these things and I had to let them go.)

I let go of the idea that a suffering-riddled Facebook post means that someone is ready to do what it takes to feel better. Funny, right? Well, it's true. It took me years to release the people around me (both distant relationships and deeply intimate ones) from my expectation that they want to cultivate change in the ways that I am trained and guided to help with.

This is my job but I finally realized that, much like their misery is not my problem, my work is not their problem.

All of this releasing of expectations (or entire relationships when it comes to that) frees my family, friends, peers, and others to live their lives/truths and enjoy (or not) the consequences of their choices. Also, it frees me to live in peace.

When I release them, I free myself. I get to spend my energy playing in my own sandbox. Not only is it as clean as I left it, but it's mine. Every ounce of energy I spend playing in the sandbox of my own life is effective because this is the only place that's actually mine to tend.

All of these messy, old, codependent behaviors are being released, which puts my power back to work for me. In my life, my energy goes a long way toward building dreams and being a force of love in the world. When I keep it here, instead of wasting it trying to get other people to act (my version of) "right," truth reigns and everybody wins.

We Are Afraid That Without Our Things, We Will Cease To Exist

Any intelligent fool can make things bigger, more complex, and more violent. It takes a touch of genius — and a lot of courage — to move in the opposite direction.

- Albert Einstein

So, here we are... you and me. We've made our lives big, complex, and violent and I'm assuming we can agree that it's not working. Aren't you relieved that we both possess the touch of genius and courage necessary for us to move in the opposite direction?

Yes, we do.

Seriously, we do. Don't argue with me. I know things!

For one, I know that we are far more amazing than we realize.

I know that our lives have become so big because we were finding our way to this moment, to this place at this exact time where the new way of being could reveal itself to us. I know that we've cultivated such complexity because we needed it to survive the past, and that the time has come for us to leave all of that behind.

I know that we are a product of those who contributed our DNA, plus every experience we've had up until this moment. I know that some of those experiences were hard, harder than we even know how to wrap our brains around... not to mention all that we've done and will continue to do to heal our hearts.

See? I know things.

I know that the most violent aspect of our lives is the way that we treat ourselves and that because we are violent with ourselves, we are violent with one another.

I know we are stuck, that the life force energy is restricted in a way that threatens our lives, at the very least our livelihood. The flow has been diminished to a mere trickle by the lifetime of history archived in our bodies, and in our collective body. This junk is clouding our minds, and consuming our physical spaces. It is as if the inner walls of the pipes that carry all good things to us are lined with sludge, allowing only the minimum we need to survive to make its way into our lives.

We are simply surviving, barely enough energy to get through each day. Not enough to make the changes we long to make. Not enough to be the ones we know we were born to be. We feel it in our bodies, so heavy and stiff. Our minds are overwhelmed, attention is strained, and then there is the depression. Our hearts ache for things we dare not even wish for, as the money is not there and when it is, we fear a future without it.

Our space is closing in on us, the stuff is everywhere and we can't bring ourselves to part with it because there's too little time or attention or perhaps... it's the fear again.

We're afraid our feelings will be hurt when we long for this thing and it's gone, or when the giver realizes we've parted with their gift. We're afraid we will forget the joy of that day without the souvenir. We're afraid without that thing to anchor where we've been or who we are... that we will cease to exist.

We are afraid that without our things, we will cease to exist.

We're afraid we'll need it. We know this thing is useful and that someday we may need it and that if we release it today, we'll suffer from the lack of it... someday.

We're afraid we'll miss something in that book or magazine or paper or email or recording or whatever other clutter we've amassed that promises to help us turn this all around.

We want desperately to turn our lives around.

We want to be free, free to be the ones who have space enough to play and dream, to love and laugh, to heal and explore our own possibility and the possibilities of the lives around ours. We want to dream of living our own lives, instead of dreaming about running away to be who we believe the others to be.

We want to be free.

We can go about it a thousand ways. Of course, we already know that. It's part of the stuck-ness. We are overwhelmed. If it's weight we want to lose, we already know about the countless approaches that have worked for someone else, the experts, the programs, and ways to invest in them.

There's so much information about everything. It is absolutely paralyzing. It doesn't matter what change we want to make, there are many choices. Our brains do all of the talking, calculating, negotiating... so much that we've forgotten the sound of our own heartbeat. We've forgotten to listen to the truth of who we are, our heart song falls unnoticed upon our own preoccupied ears.

It doesn't have to be this way.

Remember, I know things and somewhere deep down inside... you know these things too.

All that you will ever be, you were on the day you were born. Nothing outside of you gives you value beyond what lives within you. Nothing out here in the world makes you who you are.

There is no need to cling.

Release those things back to the universe, to the natural flow, so others who need them today can have them, and those empty spaces will fill with the magic that lives inside of you. Give yourself the most sacred gift, the gift of space, the freedom to live what is within you… and all that you long for will flow to you. All that you need will be within your reach at the moment that you need it, now and always.

I trust you. I believe in you. I believe that you can be what you need every single day in the future without the weight of your inventory.

There is another way. A simpler way. It's not my way, my program, my idea… it's yours. Let me show you how the answers are within you. It won't cost you a thing, but it will give you everything — access to you, your answers, your intuition, your integrity.

I know that you are the courageous genius you need to be to move forward into the life of your dreams.

Can You Imagine Your Home Being Filled With Toxic Soup?

Don't own so much clutter that you will be relieved to see your house catch fire.

- Wendell Berry

Here comes another natural disaster to assist us in the releasing of our possessions. While the winds have lost some of their power, it's the flooding that we've been warned will do the most harm. People have been ordered to evacuate but, of course, not all who were encouraged to flee will actually leave.

Honestly, I don't get it. Don't you own a television or see a newspaper every once in a while? Don't you remember the hurricanes, tornadoes, wildfires, etc., that have come before this? Doesn't Mother Nature always come out on top? The Today Show's Al Roker spoke with the surfer who decided it was too intense for her but whose friends were still kicking it up in the background. Another reporter interviews a woman who doesn't "think it's going to be that bad," and has prepared by, "hoping for the best." Good luck with that.

All the talk takes me back to May of 2010 when it rained in Nashville, hard and fast, for two days, and flooded nearly everything. People died. Entire neighborhoods were under water. The symphony hall and its neighbors, all right in the middle of downtown, were conquered with ease. It was shocking to see in real life what I'd watched only on television before. We were lucky at home. So we loaded the family, cleaning supplies, and a few tools into the car, and took off in search of a way to be useful.

We stopped at one heavily impacted house to see if we could help, and they sent us down the street to check on a single mother who'd lost everything. Luckily, a crew of eager sorority sisters had already come, rocked it, and moved on. All that remained, the owner and her children had to do on their own.

The process of picking up every single item you own to make a decision about its fate is daunting but at some point, that is what has to be done. She sent us down the street to another woman whose house and barn had also been inundated with flood water. She said, "While they were trying to escape, her husband had a heart attack and he's in the hospital. She doesn't have any family here and I think she probably needs you even more than I do."

We found a lovely, overwhelmed, and in fact, alone woman talking on a cell phone in the middle of her absolutely wasted house. She whispered, "Someone is here. I'll call you back." She was confused that we just popped up out of nowhere asking to help her. We recognized the woman's overwhelm, and suggested beginning outside, perhaps pulling items to the curb that the water brought in from elsewhere so that neighbors might recognize their coolers, chairs, planters, etc. and take them home. I remember that she was concerned about our safety. Everything for miles was either covered in a layer of toxic dust or still had that awful-smelling water pooled inside (plus there was the poison ivy under the pine trees). We reassured her we would be careful, and asked her to yell when she was ready for help inside. Still visibly shaken, we let her be for a while, all aware that she'd been violated. She was traumatized. It was humbling.

Later she explained her confused shock, "Earlier today, I was on the phone with my friend who lives far away and can't come help. I was upset, and didn't know what to do. She listened to me for a while and then asked if there was anything she could do to help. I laughed and said, 'I don't know. Can you post something on the Internet that says we need a motorcycle gang at this address?'" That was the conversation we'd interrupted.

We were her motorcycle gang.

If you're at home, look around you. Imagine your house being filled with toxic soup. Imagine having to either clean (like seriously-disinfect-or-face-life-threatening-illness clean) or dispose of every single thing you own — closets, basement, garage, cabinets, bathroom, bookcases, office, etc. Everything. I couldn't imagine until I stood there and watched that woman live it.

And although she'd been reassured that he would recover, her husband remained hospitalized for some time. Like many in the area, they did not have flood insurance. The house would need to be completely gutted and everything within had to be removed. We did what we could to support her for the next few days. It was a huge, humbling wake-up call for me, both personally and professionally, around the relationship between us — people, especially Americans — and our stuff. Wild, isn't it? One day you're trying to decide how you'll ever properly manage the circus of leftovers (a constant when you're only cooking for two) if you part with even one of these Tupperware containers. Next thing you know, you and a faux motorcycle gang member have agreed that out of that entire cabinet, two of the bowls and their corresponding lids can be washed and packed to go to the temporary shelter. The rest can go.

Friends who volunteered elsewhere reported much of the same from all over town. Appliances were sent to the landfill. Overstuffed pantries that home-owners "never could get around to cleaning out," were now easily emptied. Canned goods (that hadn't expired) were donated to the food bank and the rest was just trash. Lots of treasured possessions were destroyed in the chaos, and lots of what wasn't destroyed molded soon anyway. Clothes that hadn't been worn in years couldn't be donated because they were filthy, and such dramatic recovery efforts rarely include time and money to wash laundry. It's all just thrown away.

Think of all the time we spend trying to deal with our clutter, all the fuss and resistance that keeps us stuck. We are consumed with indecision about the stuff in our space. We cling, collect, and gather. Can you imagine the energy that goes into the relationship between us and our stuff? And still, in a flash... all of those things are trash, an enormous burden to the earth.

Late on the second day, the woman wished aloud that she'd released all of that stuff years ago. Then she whispered that while she would never have asked for this flood, part of her was grateful for the clarity. She felt as if she was finally able to free herself from all of it.

Since I started sharing these ideas and method with my clients, I've heard several people wish for a well-placed match. Many more have wished someone would come carry everything inside their homes out to the front yard so they could bring back in only what they wanted to keep. The idea of having to go about it the other way around overwhelms and that's completely understandable.

Sometimes it takes a lot of work to heal something that's broken. But the healing part doesn't have to suck. We can enjoy taking back our lives but the recovery must be intense enough to cultivate a change within us, to keep us from continuing to accumulate excessively. It must be challenging enough to help us release that which no longer serves us.

When we've lived beyond our means, corrective action must be taken to move back into alignment with the life that is true for us. When we overspend, we have to pay it back. When we overeat, we have to lose the weight. When we take in more than our space can host (without compromising 'the thing called life' that our space is intended for), then we have to do something in order to get back on track.

And certainly, a disaster will occasionally swoop in to assist this process but it isn't necessary (and it's terrible to go through it). Without being fully engaged in the releasing of our possessions (plus the emotions those things represent), we won't be changed enough to keep from going there again. I once had a client who'd lost everything in a tornado a few years before we began working together. They'd rebuilt and she was mortified to realize that what had previously taken years to accumulate had been re-accumulated in a fraction of that time. Her story opened my eyes to the importance of choice in clutter clearing.

We have to be in choice, even if it's a crisis that offers us that choice — fire, natural disaster, divorce, etc. She'd had her home and its contents taken from her. Other people came, salvaged the few items and tossed the rest. She didn't have to choose to release these things, and she experienced no healing of the wounds that caused the clutter to accumulate in the beginning.

Clearing out our clutter by choice — whether triggered by chaos or something completely different — is an incredibly therapeutic, truly healing act of personal evolution. The difference lives, as is always the case, within us. It's all about the choice.

Are you in choice here, or do you feel like a victim? Are you in control of the things you can control? Are you learning from the lessons being offered in this situation? Are you allowing this life-changing situation to change you?

And, perhaps most importantly: Do you need to wait for a disaster to give you this choice or do you have the courage to make this choice for yourself?

Is Your Clutter Clinical?

One woman has her attic packed so tightly that she wonders if some day she'll come home to find all that stuff on her living room floor. Another swears that the cabinets in her kitchen are holding her favorite cookware hostage. She won't let her daughter open the coat closet for fear that the landslide of this-is-so-handies, here-for-nows, assorted-what-nots, and I-remember-whens might flatten her only child. Meanwhile, another claims she'll dispatch a SWAT team to rub me out if I ever show anyone the pictures she took of her house this morning and emailed to prove that she has clutter.

We are living beyond our means. Yes, I said beyond our means, just like the federal government (in the

United States, at least), spending more than we have to spend. Only instead of money, we're overspending our space. I once believed that I needed space to hold my stuff, that if I had more stuff than would fit in my space, I could get more space. It meant bigger places, more closets, more cabinets, more storage. And if that couldn't be attained, the whole off-site storage industry popped up to reinforce that it's not just normal but often necessary to possess more than our space will hold.

I have since learned that my space is for living my life, not just storing my stuff, and all that stuff was keeping me from actually living in my space. I spent so much time managing that stuff that I wasn't managing my actual life. Yesterday, a friend said, "There's so much stuff in this space, I don't have room to have a party or paint with my kids or dance. There's no room for us to play!"

Instead of playing, we've been played. That thing we were doing all this time wasn't playing or living or loving or healing. They call it shopping, and beyond the basics, it's essentially a mind-numbing waste of precious resources (time, money, energy, attention, and perhaps most importantly in this conversation, space). Shopping is mind-numbing, which we attempt to use to distract ourselves from the realities of fear, pressure, unmet needs, and whatever else ails us. But look around. Is it working as well as you hoped?

I bet the manufacturers, retailers, marketers, and advertisers of the world released a massive, collective sigh of relief on the day that whole off-site storage thing took off. Our houses were full to the brim and the banks wouldn't let us buy bigger houses because we'd shopped all of our money and credit away. It looked as if the shopping spree might actually finally be coming to an end but thank goodness they came to the rescue. Now, we just out-source our stuff, instead of actually dealing with it.

We make room in our kitchen by moving not-so-regularly-used kitchen stuff to shelves in the garage, space that became available when we took the not-so-regularly-used garage stuff down the street to Pay Us To Babysit The Stuff You Don't Need Anymore, LLC, or whatever that place is called.

When I first started teaching space healing work-shops, the registration emails were full of excitement and inspired commitments, mixed with heartbreak. A few of them were straight-up shocking.

So far, the smallest space was a sailboat (home to a family of five!) and the largest had 5 bedrooms and a pool house. The spaces are everything from meticulously clean and organized mounds of clutter to what we might call mainstream or normative clutter. A few are just this side of the qualifying for one of those shows about hoarding and may need more help than I can offer. This is a reality that any decent professional is prepared for in a situation like this. It would be cruel and unusual punishment to reel someone in with serene stock photos and dramatic promises when we might be talking about a situation more serious than can be helped with a month of emails, 2-minute video tips, expert interviews, and group calls.

You will never hear me say that this book or one of my workshops is all you will ever need to change your life forever. I refuse to risk leaving you feeling like a failure to secure myself a spot in the expert panel. We must be gentle with ourselves while making these changes. (That's not to be confused with 'easy on ourselves,' don't get excited!)

Clutter (like our bodies and our money) represents our innermost state of being. Lots of old emotions are tied up in those belongings. We want them gone but we don't, or at least we don't know how.

Sometimes we feel too embarrassed to speak of the reality of our situation. Clutter (or extra weight or financial challenges) seem to attract more of the same. Add in the shame and soon we're alone (or at least we feel alone), suffering, and unwilling to ask for the support we need to make a change.

Is your clutter clinical?

The truth is that I don't know. That's for you to decide. (Or, I suppose, for others to decide if you're seriously impaired but that's not the kind of extreme I'm talking about here.) There are stories of people with little or no support who've changed their lives dramatically, while other people with the world at their fingertips sometimes can't seem to turn it around. People talk to me all the time about how they want to change something — lose weight, leave the relationship or job, pursue a dream, clear the clutter, whatever — but can't decide if they need to hire me (or someone like me) or not. I say this, "If you want to do it, do it. If you want to do it... and can't, then get yourself the support you need and do it."

It always comes back to that same issue. Can you do it? Not "should" you be able to do it? Not do you want to do it? The question is, can you do it?

If you can't, can you do it with an accountability partner? That's when two people (or more, if it makes sense) working on similar goals, agree to be a source of accountability to one another. They will check in, probably daily at least in the most intense parts of the journey, to report what they intend to do each day to move toward their respective goals, and also that they actually did it. They can share resources and brainstorm together when someone has a challenge they can't solve alone. People who need this level of support might want to share this chapter with their people adding, "Who wants to do this with me?" Ideas, inspiration, and accountability will be enough for some to get it done.

If that's not enough, can you do it with the support of someone who has already won the game you want to play? If you know someone who has already done this, ask how they did it. They might be willing and able to support you during this time. Also, 12-step programs are wonderful and welcoming places to get support, depending on the change you'd like to make. I know a few people who've had success working with mentors or spiritual/religious types of advisers.

If not, can you do it with professional support, like a life coach, intuitive guide, or spiritual teacher?

That would be me, or someone like me, whose job it is to support people throughout transformations like the one you're ready to make. Everyone has a different style and method, and you want to find someone that feels right in your gut. You want to think, "Yes, this one is for me." Yes, it costs money to work with most of us. It's what we do for a living. The key is: Many of us are worth what you will pay us… if you do your part.

Sometimes, even working with me one-on-one isn't going to work. If you don't really want to make the change, it's not going to work. So, don't hire a professional for your daughter-in-law so she'll be a better wife to your son. I tell people that giving me as a gift is a lot like giving a vacuum cleaner. It basically says, "Your life is a mess and it's making my life a mess, too." It rarely goes well. Of course, there are exceptions to that rule. For example, if someone wants to work with me, is ready to do the work, and asks for the gift, we have a pretty good chance of being productive in our time together. To be successful, you have to find a motivation that is true for you and powerful enough to keep you moving when you come face to face with your own fears, frustration, and resistance.

In fact, some of the people who've picked up this book may not be clear about their goals, which is essential, so you've got to find that motivation and anchor it before you go any further.

And, there are times that even if my client really wants it and they're giving it their all, just the two of us working together isn't enough. I've referred clients out to therapists before proceeding with our work together. I've encouraged some of them to supplement our work with 12-step program work. A handful of my clients have been working with both a therapist and me at the same time; a powerful duo when that's what the client needs to be fully supported.

The key to making changes is being fully supported. Once again, the key to making changes is being fully supported. The question now becomes... are you prepared to get the support you need to make this change? If the answer is yes, then you can do it.

This might just mean talking to the people you live with to express your desires for a more healthy space. It might mean asking your loved ones to join you on this journey. If they are resistant, don't assume that means this journey is impossible. Keep reading and we'll talk more about resistant house-mates a little later.

If clutter is your thing, if you are living beyond your physical means, then say yes to this process and then... freaking DO IT. If it's not about clutter, then say yes to whatever it is that you need to make this change and then DO IT.

Just... do it? I know, that's so Nike. What's a cheesy, people-loving Unruly Woman to do when those are the words that fall onto the keyboard?

Challenge

Head to your bedroom closet. Find 27 things that no longer serve you. Release them.

I know this seems random. It's the first challenge we do in every workshop. There's something really tender about the stuff we find in our bedroom closets. It's one of the most hidden places in the room in our homes that is supposed to be just for us. And our relationships with our bodies are really tied up in the clothes. Trust me on this one. Head to the closet and dig in.

Make Projects Possible or Let Them Go

I purchased the absolutely perfect red paint to transform the front door into the warm and welcoming entry of my dreams... about a year ago. Yes, I'm serious. One. Year. Ago. I crack myself up.

My plan for today included writing about knocking some projects off of my "to do" list. I searched my brain for the best, most universally applicable examples of projects. I hummed and pondered and wondered, trying to come up with projects that students already mentioned they needed to tend. I had nothing, nothing at all!

And then I thought, if I had projects to do, what would they be?

(Insert laughter.)

In a blink, I had a dozen on my page. I'm the one hosting this space healing adventure and that list had me wondering if I ever get anything done. Of course, I do. I'm rather productive but the same stuff, usually that which is just on the edge of my comfort zone, gets put off over and over again. There's always plenty of stuff that's easy to do (or practically on fire), so why would I stop to do a project that's resting so comfortably on the back burner?

My job is a big, fat piece of humble pie. Every single time I think I'm helping someone else, I realize that the lesson I offered them is for me, too. It seems that they are always for me. When I offer support to someone else, the message comes back and slaps me in the face. Gently, at first but if I don't pull it together pretty quickly things get out of hand.

So, guess what I planned to do today? Yes, it's time to paint that door. I also decided (and committed) to clear out some junk from the trunk (of my car), to attempt to repair the hole in my son's new favorite t-shirt, and package up a few thank-you gifts for clients.

I know how easy it is for projects to get piled up. In fact, at my house, they aren't even piled up. They are more spread out here and there, a little in each room, side by side. That's because everyone who lives here has some degree of anxiety about forgetting things. There's a little voice in our heads that tells us that if we can't see it, we won't do it.

Well, guess what? If we don't dedicate the resources — time, money, energy, etc. — we don't do it anyway! And before long, the first begins to blend into the rest of them and we find ourselves with clutter and to-do list drama.

Of course, there is good news. I always have some, right? And it's always basically the same.

It doesn't have to be this way.

I (and you) aren't stuck here but, there is only one way out. It's the same as everything else we will deal with here in my world. We have to stop and deal with our stuff, which of course means dealing with ourselves. It takes making a decision that we are unwilling to let another day close without bringing this situation to a resolution.

Period.

That may mean:

- Grabbing a screwdriver

- Going to the store for supplies

- Calling the credit card company to make payment arrangements

- Sitting down to sort the pictures

- Reading the damn magazines

- Searching the Internet for a fix

To get it done, we have to decide on the necessary action… and then, we have to take it. Make no mistake, both parts are equally important.

Step One: Decide what needs to be done

I find it's very useful to have break it down into small steps, each with a verb and a noun. So, instead of adding "Clean house," to my list, I might say:

- Clean upstairs bathroom

- Clean downstairs bathroom

- Change out towels

- Wash laundry

- Put laundry away

- Vacuum upstairs

- Vacuum downstairs

- Vacuum the stairs (I don't love that part.)

- Mop kitchen floor

I can add the other elements, like dusting and cleaning the windows, and make a comprehensive list. This detailed approach helps me for a number of reasons. First, I have days that I'm so overwhelmed by the realities of that list that I can't remember what "clean house" actually means. I just walk in circles — frustrated with my life and my house and myself — until I remember that I have a laptop with an Internet connection to help lull me back to sleep. Sucker. On those days, I need actionable items (the noun/verb combo is powerful. Do this to your list!).

Basically, I need my list to boss me around.

Second, I am checklist obsessed. It's true, I am. I love the sense of accomplishment that comes from saying to the piece of paper that's bossing me around, "I did that! What's next?" There is something about the way my brain works, something related to the thing they call ADHD, that keeps me from experiencing the natural euphoria that normally follows accomplishment. I don't get the surge of happy feelings that I read about in my Intro to Psych textbook. No high at all, just moving on. Checking the items off of that list forces me to see what I've accomplished. It anchors my success for me and I promise, that's a good thing.

Third, I wander off. It's pretty bad. I sometimes feel sorry for my people because I love them. I really do, and living with me isn't so easy. If my first born was up on the roof, needing a hammer, it may not be a safe bet to send me to fetch one. Yes, sometimes it is that serious.

On my way to the shed to get the hammer, I'd see the empty bird feeder. So, I'd fetch the seeds from the pantry to fill that up and then, I'd notice the tomatoes that are ripe and I'd pick them. Thinking they'd be nice on a salad, I'd notice that it was almost lunch time and I'd head into the kitchen to prepare a feast. Of course, then I'd see that we are out of cucumbers… and oh, how I just love cucumbers on my salad. So naturally, I'd go to the store.

And, there's a good chance I might not even notice that I knocked the ladder over when I backed out of my parking spot, leaving my charming young son on the roof without a hammer, or a way down. You see how easy it is to lose a girl like me? Like I said, I wander off. Those who love me know about it and plan accordingly. But, I'm in charge of the everyday maintenance of my distracted self. The list keeps me on track. Without it, I can look up and realize that it's already tomorrow.

Step Two: Do it

It's that simple. If you're feeling stuck and there are any projects hanging out among the stacks of clutter, then you have to decide what to do… and do it. If there are lots of projects, then you have to repeat the first two steps over and over until it's all nice in your world again. See? Isn't this fun?

Oh, there's one more thing. Sometimes, it's not worth it. Not. Freaking. Worth. It.

My son's otherwise still new-looking shirt is worth the energy it's going to take me to fix it, if I can. (Update: I rocked that shirt, by the way.) My pants, which also have a hole, are tired and old and not worth it to me. Sometimes, I create the time necessary to catch up on the magazines and sometimes I simply remind myself that "what goes around, comes around" works especially well for magazines. It allows me to release them, knowing that any precious thing I need to know will come back to me in another issue or by some other form.

Sometimes, I decide that it's just not worth it to keep saying I am going to do a project. I could simply walk away from the whole door painting thing and I find a new home for the paint. Not this time, of course: that door is going to be red. Period. But, I've done it before. If you don't have the resources to do something you'd previously committed to doing, just bail. Call it done.

The key here is to do it or don't but, if you're not going to do this project in a timely manner… let it go.

Today, I made a box for all of my crafty projects. It has a scarf that got hard, so I wandered off, and a hat that I can't figure out how to finish, so I wandered off. Also, there's a big bowl/basket made of recycled blue jeans that I want to take apart to make three smaller bowls/baskets, and a quilt I mean to tie dye. I put them all in this box and labeled it with an expiration date one month from today.

This will keep the "I meant to…," from going on forever. Otherwise, it will. I know this because I've met me before. If I want a different outcome, I've got to do something different.

Step One: Decide what needs to be done. Step Two: Do it. Got it?

Challenge

Complete one project on your to do list, or decide not to and be rid of it! Then, repeat, repeat, repeat... as many times as you can stand it!

If you don't have a list written of all of your projects, that can be today's project too.

Craft an Exit Strategy

Release. Release. Release.

This approach is about releasing that which no longer serves you from your physical environment. Most of the stories in this book are about how to shift your relationship with stuff enough to recognize what no longer serves you, so you'll be willing to release it.

To be clear, the stuff that isn't serving you already doesn't serve you. This is about recognizing it, which is by far the most challenging part of the shift.

The other part is getting that stuff out of your house. This too can be a challenge which we discuss later. For now, here are some important factors to consider when you're making a plan.

How to do the Challenges

Time and Energy. We have to actually make the time to do the challenges each day. If you're too busy, or too drained, the reality is that nothing I can write on these pages will make this change possible. You have to make room in your day to physically do this. The good news is that unless your situation is extreme, it's not actually all that crazy of a commitment.

Decisions. We have to be able to decide if we need this (insert thing) or not, over and over again for everything in your space. I suggest asking of each item, "Does this item serve me more than the space it occupies would serve me?" Basically, what we all want is more space to breathe, think, and live, and as far as I'm concerned, every item is auditioning for a sacred spot in my house.

Means. We have to have the physical strength to carry this stuff away, or some other means of having it carried away for us. (It is important to ask for help if you lack the energy or strength to do it alone). We probably need to have something to put this stuff in to carry it away — trash bags, boxes, bins, etc.

Destination. We have to do something with this stuff, as stacking it up by the back door isn't quite far enough away to provide any freedom. Some will inevitably be trash but think 'recycle, reuse, repurpose' whenever possible. Finding someone who can use that which no longer serves you (clutter) can be one of the most rewarding aspects of clearing your space

Sell or Share. We fill our space, sometimes even accidentally, with stuff because of our perception of it as valuable. Sometimes we have the time and energy, decision-making skills, means, and a destination, and we still struggle to let go of the value of that stuff. It can be difficult to release the possibility of receiving money in exchange for our possessions, especially if our life is underfunded.

If so, we must to either invest more time, energy, decisions, and means to find a destination that's willing to pay for our stuff. Or we must decide to let it go. We can chose to have a yard sale, estate sale, find a dealer or collector of that stuff, or to post it online for sale ourselves. We can even try find someone to do it for us and split the profit. Those options each require different resources — time, energy, brain power, etc. — and unless you're prepared to carry that out in a short term way (my guidance for people is by the end of the month in question), it's best to just release it.

It's tempting to skip creation of your exit strategy but taking time to think through these factors (and talk through options with housemates if you live with others) will dramatically impact the results you cultivate. Yes, the results. You are taking action, or at least considering it, and you want to get the most bang for each energetic buck. You deserve to feel deep freedom, not just whatever you can squeeze out with the tools and habits of the people who raised you.

You are worth whatever it takes to move back into alignment with your true, powerful self.

Challenge

Let's test your exit strategy! Find 27 things from anywhere in your house to donate to wherever you can donate things and do it... now. It can be clothing, household goods, food, toys your children (or you) have out-grown. Find 27 and find a good home for them. Go!

What If It Hurts
to Let Go?

We've talked about releasing responsibly and you've learned how to craft an effective exit strategy. I fancied those a fabulous foundation and frankly, was quite pleased with myself. (Note the premature confidence, falling on just this side of completely self-destructive arrogance. Cue doom music... and probably a giggle or two from those who know me well enough to know this isn't the first time that music has been cued.)

Let's talk about the hurt.

About a week into my first space healing program, I started getting comments, emails, and phone calls from students about the pain that was coming up around this process. A few examples of this include: condolence cards from a when a parent died, decades worth of statements representing a significant financial inheritance, clothes and food that were donated in a time of great need (but don't actually serve them), and the extraordinary amounts of goods acquired when it was easier to shop… than to feel.

"What if getting rid of something makes me sad? Does that mean I should keep it? Decluttering my divorce papers/stuff felt very freeing. However, I am finding it difficult to get rid of a magazine the doctor's office gave me when I was pregnant. I miscarried and it has sat down in my basement collecting dust for seven years. Since my divorce four years ago when I have tried to declutter the basement, I always think about getting rid of it, but keep it. I always figured some day when I was having a baby I would need it. This weekend when I chose to declutter the basement, ironically it was the first thing I put in my box to go. As I continued with my decluttering I started getting sad at the thought of getting rid of it. I feel like it means I will never have my dream of having my own family. I decided to sit on it for a few

days to think about it. I don't think I really want it any more, but question if it's healthy to toss it, since I feel like I'm giving up on my dreams. I had several other baby things, that I gave to friends and family as they had babies. I figured I wasn't using them now, so someone else may as well get use out of them. So I'm not quite sure of the hold this magazine seems to have on me."

- Annie

"What if getting rid of something makes me sad?"

It's not usually the releasing of a specific item that makes us sad, it's that considering releasing the item reminds us how a powerful life experience made us feel. It's not letting go of the magazine that makes you sad, it's that the magazine reminds you of the baby you lost and that's terribly sad. That's why we cling to things, releasing them makes us remember the feeling associated with it. As we release the item, we release more layers of the pain. If we keep the item, we continue to experience the pain. Even if we have it packed away, it's never truly out of our consciousness. It has its hook in you, draining you.

"Does that mean I should keep it?"

Ultimately, the goal here is to own only those things that we use or truly love. We want to be surrounded by things that feel good to us. You certainly can keep anything until you're ready to release it but I'm not a fan of "should" for anything. And I certainly wouldn't advise anyone to keep anything that has a painful association. That is the opposite of the progress, the freedom, we are seeking here.

"Since my divorce four years ago when I have tried to declutter the basement, I always think about getting rid of it, but keep it. I always figured some day when I was having a baby I would need it."

When you have a baby, you will need support, information, and inspiration… and you will receive it, just as this magazine came to you with such ease before. This one is for the baby you lost. You won't need it for the next child. Your loss is undeniable, painful, and a million other things that I recognize only in the way that another woman who's lost a child in her womb can know. That magazine represents that life and the loss of it, but the magazine is not that life or that loss, and releasing it will free you, not from having had a miscarriage, but from clinging to the loss in a way that holds you back.

"I feel like it means I will never have my dream of having my own family."

I gently, lovingly, and respectfully ask that you consider this statement again… is it true that releasing this magazine will keep you from having a baby? Or that it will keep you from remembering that you want to have a baby? I imagine that your response is something like, "of course not."

Is there something different, perhaps something more true and consistent with your actual feelings about this life and loss, that you can do to honor the memory this magazine represents? I've heard of many different ideas (for example planting a tree, writing a letter and releasing it by fire, wind, earth, or water, etc.) and would be honored to explore some of them with you, if you'd like.

I understand now that there is a sixth element I neglected before, and it must be tended in order for us to release these things that no longer serve us. I'm seeing it over and over again, this paralysis between the spirit and stuff. The reason that stuff is here, occupying the space we need to breathe and think and live, is that it causes us discomfort to release it. It causes us discomfort to even consider releasing it, or perhaps even to consider it at all. So, we try not to.

We put it in our basements and our attics. We stuff it in the closet and close the door. We spend our entire lives trying to find a way to manage our stuff — buying more organizing materials, searching for "better" housekeeping ideas, and beating ourselves up for failing to keep our stuff in order. That's managing our stuff, instead of managing our lives.

The stuff is locked into the feelings and the feelings are locked into the stuff. It doesn't matter from which side we break the lock. What matters is that we break it. When we have the courage to say, "I'm sick of being stuck," and begin this process of releasing those things that no longer serve us, every-thing becomes possible.

It works because dealing with our clutter is simply a willingness to, at long last, deal with ourselves.

Challenge

Look for one thing that hurts but that you know it's time to release. Let it go.

The Ins and Outs of Clutter Clearing

I knew that coming between people and their stuff, or at least delivering messages that made it look like I wanted to, was going to be tricky. I knew there would be a fight. I begged and pleaded to the powers that be to show me how to serve, what I could do to be a "major player in the loving transformation of the world." I wanted this assignment. Then when it came in, I freaked out.

Here is what I heard: Prepare them to travel lightly through what lies ahead by releasing attachments to things and old wounds.

After working as a professional organizer off and on for 10 years, I transitioned into life coaching with pure delight that my trash-bag-holding days were over. It's not that I didn't love that work. I really loved it. In fact, clutter clearing is like play for me and it goes all the way back to childhood. But my organizing client's results were disheartening; only about a third of the clients never needed me again. That may sound like a bad marketing perspective but truly, I wanted people to heal what caused them to attract those conditions. I didn't want them to continue to need to work with me; they deserved a better way of life.

As with calories and weight, the health of our space depends both on what comes in and goes out. To keep a nice, stable, physical environment, we want to strive for balance, to have enough space within the walls in question — whether it's 400 square feet or 12,000 square feet, a single room or multiple homes, to hold our possessions and to live. This is about living within our means, not just storing our stuff. We need space to live — room to relax and play, dance and learn, love and grow, breathe and feel — and if our space is full to the brim with stuff, it seems to me that we're not living well.

The basics are simple. If the space is empty, then there is room to receive incoming goods. Once the equation is balanced, meaning that there is enough room for the stuff AND the living that needs to take place in that space, it's important to find a new 'stuff strategy' to keep that balance. After finding a healthy balance in the clothes closet, for example, some people commit to an even exchange strategy. This means that for every incoming piece of clothing, you choose an outgoing item in exchange.

It turns out, I don't hear from a lot of people whose lives are balanced. I'm a resource for people who want to change their lives. People call me when the scales are tipped so far in one direction or the other that they can't get it back on their own. And once you're out of balance, continuing what got you here doesn't usually keep the situation stable. These out-of-whack (note the highly technical expert lingo) habits and behaviors cultivate a growing sense of dissatisfaction, shame, and frustration which result in more of the unproductive habits and behaviors. It doesn't take long before we have ourselves a downward spiral.

These situations get worse over time, and making a change becomes more and more difficult with each new development. That's when I get a call or an email, "I want to change. I really do but nothing I try works… it seems like every step forward comes with four steps back. I don't even know where to start." It doesn't matter which area of life is out of balance, once there is too much coming in (as with calories and stuff) or too much going out (as with spending or energy), something has to give.

It takes new habits and behaviors to maintain a healthy way of living, combined with some corrective action to bring the out of control situation back into balance. Once we have extra weight, we can't just start consuming and burning the same number of calories and expect to lose weight. We have to burn more than we consume to release the extra weight. The same concept applies to everything. We have to bring in more money than we spend in order to pay off debt. And once our house is filled past the point of comfort, one thing out for everything that comes in will not result in balance.

To find balance in an overwhelmed physical space, to make room to truly live, more has to go out than is coming in.

Once more for clarity: *Reduce incoming. Increase outgoing.*

I've never met anyone, not one single person, who had trouble with only one side of this equation. In order to free ourselves from chaos, we must be willing to explore both sides.

What is all of this stuff? Where is it coming from? How does it get here? Why did I purchase these things? How do I feel when I shop online? What makes me go to the thrift store four days a week? Why can't I just wear the clothes that I already have? Why am I afraid to be without a kitchen full of food at all times? What would happen if I came straight home after work instead of going shopping?

Why do I have so many clothes that I don't even wear? Why am I afraid to open my mail? How come nobody else wanted to keep all of mother's things when we cleaned out the house after she died and why do I still have them in my living room? Why can't I throw that thing away? What do I think will happen if I recycle all of these magazines instead of trying to find time to read them?

The list of questions I've asked people about their stuff could go on for days. There are two sides to the story of your stuff, and it's important to look at them both. Why is so much coming in and what needs to heal for you to be willing to reduce that?

Then, what prevents you from releasing things from your physical environment that no longer serve you? And again, it takes digging into why you're hanging on to those things. This is about exposing the loss or wound or insecurity or fear or, on rare occasions, the positive memory that allows that thing to keep its hook in you. Once you can see the hook, you can gently remove it, and let that thing go for good.

What has its hooks in you? Do you feel stuck? Look around your physical environment, can you see signs there that something is out of balance? What's going on? What kind of support do you need?

What did reading this chapter bring up for you?

Challenge

It's time for an expiration date purge! Grab a trash bag and go through the bathroom, kitchen, and anywhere else you might find stuff with expiration dates and release, release, release anything that is past the expiration date.

Use It or Lose It

I don't care much for stuff, never have really. And while I'd like to tell you that it's because I'm all zen or I try to have less and live more... that would be a lie. The truth is I have something just this side of a phobia about stuff. It's not all stuff actually, it's unused stuff that makes me crazy.

For example, I'd be quite pleased to have this drum kit in my kitchen, if someone would play the damned thing.

No seriously. I would. It would thrill me. But, despite my certainty that the boy who's been drumming since before he could walk would love, love, love to have drums when I scored them at a yard sale two summers ago, he does not, in fact, play these drums. Nobody is drumming here, not even occasionally, and for now, at least, that makes the drums unused.

When you have a two bedroom condominium with four people and four cats, drums in the kitchen are either an indication that a well-supported passionate musician lives here... or they are clutter.

At least that's where the line is for me: *Use it or lose it.*

It's a hard line, I know. So much so, in fact, that I occasionally pause to check in about it. I wonder if there's something wrong with me that I don't have more affection for things, that I'm not more attached.

Searching for shells is truly one of my most treasured vacation activities. It's so meditative and peaceful, a sacred insight into the beauty and magic this planet has to offer. And then, I have the shells. Each visit to the ocean leaves me more and more particular about what I bring home. The loot from the last trip, only the tiniest and most perfectly unique shells, could fit in a soap dish. I was very conservative.

Still, I've done nothing with them and so, I have three vacations worth of shells in one of those beach buckets in the game cabinet in the kitchen (like I said, it's a small place and we have to be creative). There are a few ideas, good ideas even, but I haven't D.O.N.E. anything with them.

I could pull out the tiny ones and make something artsy to hang on the wall but I already have art on the walls, and some tucked away in the closet that don't fit on the walls. Plus, there's the fact that I've been in a thrift store or two in my day and I can't seem to forget that there is always at least one of those it-was-a great-idea-but-then-a-couple-of-the-shells-fell-off-and-so-we-donated-it souvenirs from some other family's beach vacation.

Sure, I could pull them out and put some in a bowl to display. For some people, that might just be the perfect visual reminder to take them back to the heavenly time spent at the beach, to help them reconnect to that blissed out, I'm-at-one-with-the-earth feeling.

Perfect.

That's called anchoring and when used well, it's a powerful tool that can help us pull the way we felt in a powerful moment forward into our everyday lives. Please note the "when used well" part of that last statement on anchoring. Everything in our space is anchored in our bodies and our minds. Everything. Look around you. Do you want all of that anchored for you?

So the bowl of perfect shells would be anchoring something for me. I know me well enough to know that a bowl of shells will soon be a bowl of dusty shells and that is NOT going to remind me of the Zen Christy who sat on the beach a year ago. It will anchor, literally every single time I see it or think about it, that I need to dust.

Now, if the only thing sitting about in my house was this bowl of shells and say two or three other inspirational anchors, I would get the intended message. I also would have time to stop once a week and rid the shells of their dusty coating in a sink full of soapy water. Then, I could rinse them and spread them out on a clean, white, linen towel (perfectly ironed, of course) to air dry, before ceremoniously returning them to the bowl. Probably, I would even come to find that weekly ritual to be pleasurable and cathartic. It sounds lovely but it's not my truth.

That's not my house, my life, or my reality, at least for now. So, no shells will be collecting dust in the bowl. Period.

Honestly, it's a self-defensive move. It's an act of self-love to resell the yard sale drum kit. It's an act of self-love to go to the beach to spend time collecting/admiring the shells.

And, it's also loving to take pictures of our treasures, to anchor the memory of that sacred time together so I can revisit them any time I want, and then return them to the ocean. That's what I'll be doing when I go back, returning these shells, as I've come to realize that they do not serve me more than the space would serve me.

Does this item serve me more than the space it occupies would serve me?

That's the question that we must ask of every single item we own during this process. Early in the sharing of this method, one woman inquired about books as clutter. She wrote, "I have a difficult time getting rid of books, even in this new era of Internet. There's something comforting about having shelves of books...which I'll NEVER reread nor go to for reference, despite being the rationale for holding on to them. Please help! They're like wonderful old friends who are filled with positive memories."

Receiving this inquiry thrilled me, partly because lots of people have book "issues" and we need to deal with them. Another part wanted to address the specific challenge of self-help books and materials because people who have issues often surround themselves with the stuff they think will help them make a change. If you're not using it, it's clutter. Yes, even if it could help. If it's not helping, it's clutter. Yes, even if you "should" use them. If you're not, it's clutter.

The biggest part of me was excited because she asked about the one thing that I cling to. I LOVE BOOKS. In fact, I only recently made peace with releasing my death grip on books.

Books are for reading. If you're not reading them, consider letting them go. Their purpose is to entertain, inform, amuse, inspire, support, etc., and if it is not serving you more than the space the book occupies would serve you, choose the space. Open space invites refreshing, new experiences into your life. Yes, books can do the same but only if you're reading them.

Nothing refreshing and new comes to you through a closed book but it will rush into open, welcoming spaces. Let the books go.

There is something comforting about shelves of books. There is also something comforting about a glass of wine but if we drink it a bottle at a time, it's a problem. If you have more books than you have room to hold them, it's a problem. And, even if you have cases and cases to store them, is this really the way we want to be comforted? Again, holding them hostage isn't actually serving us.

Use it or lose it.

They are like old friends filled with positive memories. Maybe so, but do you have your human friends tied up in the basement because they hold all of the memories of your fine times together? If you want to remember them, write about them in your journal or take their picture, but holding them hostage is no way to show gratitude for the good times you've shared.

And, let's talk about the positive memories. You loved something, so you want to keep something to make sure you remember, and that sounds so lovely and romantic, right? It is. Until we remember that every item we own is anchoring something for us. We want to have this and keep it forever to remember but guess what else I'm hearing from you?

I'm so tired. I'm so overwhelmed. Any questions? You might be... over- anchored? The only way to reduce your chaos is to release the sources of that chaos.

This is about freeing yourself from the past so you can live in this moment, and enjoying life as it is today. We are too anchored to think straight. Our homes are full of things that remind us only of how full of things our homes are. That's it. Let it go.

Release these books so they can rock someone else's world... and I promise, you'll be freeing yourself.

Challenge

Clear your self-help clutter!

Grab a bag, box, or pick-up truck (whatever it takes) and collect all of the self-help materials into a single space. Think about books, programs, planners, organizers, systems, DVDs, meditation CDs, and on and on. Get it all!

Once you've done that, take a moment to really look at those things. Take a deep breath. Then, another. What would happen tomorrow if all that stuff had vanished? Would you have less potential? Do those materials make you a better person? What are those things saying to you?

You really should...

If only you'd try...

Read me and...

This book holds the secret to...

Lastly, there is our basic question, "Does this item serve me more than the space it occupies would serve me?"

If you are prepared to release, release, release, then go ahead and do it. If you're not, then consider this alternative experiment: Take that collection of self-helpery and store it somewhere that you won't have to deal with it for a few weeks. When that time has passed, revisit them and see what's ready to go.

Household Chaos: Why Can't I Keep It All Together?

In a world filled with gadgets, programs, containers, organizers, and cleaning products designed to help us keep our space all perfect and shiny, many of us continue to be covered up in chaos. Years ago, when I worked as a professional organizer, I saw over and over again how absolutely ineffective it is to search for an organizing solution when what you have is too much stuff.

We have too much stuff. Not all of us but most of us, and I've never met a person who needed a better way to organize their six worldly goods. Everybody is trying to organize their 30 books on a shelf that holds 18 or even 24, and it's not going to work. But, we keep searching for the special trick, or the right amount of time, or the perfect physics-defying organizing product to make it work. There just isn't one. It's either going to take more space or less stuff, and most people aren't prepared to relocate.

For me, the organizing process has always been the second step. First, we release! We let go of everything that no longer serves us. The third step is to clean. As you can imagine, the organization and cleaning become possible when we release the excess from our space. Releasing makes space healing possible.

And in the spirit of full disclosure, this isn't super-secret, crafty-Christy, organizing magic I discovered. The laws of physics have been in motion since the beginning of time. Having more stuff than you have space is a problem.

Most of the people I work with sincerely don't have enough physical space for both the stuff and the life they wish to be living. We want to be able to really live in our space, not just sleep there or sit there. What about having a dinner party? Is there room for family game night? Do you have the space to create your art or prepare food that nourishes your body? And most importantly, for me at least, is there room to dance? Just being able to pack stuff into a space doesn't mean you can actually live there.

The problem with this, of course, is that there is no industry in the less is more mentality. I mean, sure, I can make a few dollars teaching a class or writing a book about how to let go of that which no longer serves you but there's nothing to manufacture there. What about color coordinated baskets, walls of hooks, and the almighty Rubbermaid storage empire?

What will they make if we stop trying to fit our too much stuff into our homes in a way that looks pretty, makes sense, and is maintainable? Or, for that matter, what will they make if we stop buying all of that stuff in the first place? Oh, whatever, that's a battle for another time. Or is it?

People come to me because they felt stuck and most of the time their physical space is paralyzed, too. We get in this position because of two things. We have a tendency to over-consume, often in an attempt to make ourselves feel better. And we under-release, often longing for a sense of security that the stuff doesn't actually bring.

To live more in alignment with our integrity, we have to tend to both ends of that equation. First, it's about feeling what needs to be felt — and perhaps changing what needs to be changed — instead of distracting ourselves with a trip to the mall or the thrift store. And second, it's about actually maintaining our space by periodically releasing that which no longer serves us. Once that stuff-to-space ratio is balanced, organizing and cleaning are never the crises they once appeared to be.

When we live in balance, life becomes manageable. That's the bottom line we keep coming back to, isn't it? That's because it works, and we all just need something that works.

Once life is out of balance, we have to take action to recover the balance. If you're holding this book, you already know that when it comes to clearing clutter, it can be hard to get started. The daily challenges included throughout the book are designed to get you to dig into the big black hole. They are short and sweet and to the point. I tell you the space and action, freeing you from the I-don't-know-where-to-begin paralysis. These challenges are like tiny little packages of explosive that you're depositing throughout your home to break up the energy and get you moving again. But sometimes these challenges work a little too well, and people can't find their way back out of the big black hole.

"I need advice about starting and stopping a decluttering task. I find it really hard to get started, but once I start, I do not want to stop. And then keep going well past the amount of time I have, to the detriment of getting sleep. So now I am over-tired with just a few hours sleep last night. I do not want just a short spurt of energy — I want to keep going and then maintain, but I just cannot seem to have the discipline to start or stop the challenge. Advice is welcome..."

- Shelley

Certainly it makes sense to ride the waves of energy when they come. In fact, that's one of the foundational principles of this approach. Every little shift makes the next action more possible, and as we proceed the momentum builds and builds until we find ourselves back in the flow again. Riding the waves is key to our success!

Ultimately though, this is about taking back your life and if you find yourself unable to come back out of the black hole in order to care for yourself properly, that's just another kind of obstacle. And who needs more obstacles here?

If every now and then, you give up some sleep to bring something to completion, it wouldn't be uncommon. If you're always moving in a forward direction — minimizing the behaviors that created clutter to begin with — you will eventually have the backlog of clutter out of the house and won't have anything like this to get sucked into.

I've found that setting a timer is a simple trick that helps most people stay connected to life outside the big black hole. If it doesn't, then you'll want to look into why you don't want to stop. For example, are you reluctant to stop because you don't trust yourself to start again? If so, the best cure is to force yourself to stop once you've met that day's challenge and then tomorrow do it again.

We are rebuilding credibility with ourselves, moving back into alignment with our integrity. When we make promises to ourselves and break them, we lose faith in our own word. That's harsh but it's true. And just like rebuilding a relationship with someone else after we've betrayed them, we have to show we've changed. We have to be someone that we can depend on.

Remember, it's not in the huge moments of hysterical clearing that someone lives more simply forever. It's in the commitment to daily action that we free ourselves of these old ways of being.

And perhaps most importantly, if you burn yourself out, you lose. Go all in but also be loving with yourself. This is the only way to make long term, sustainable change. This is the only way to free yourself.

And you deserve to feel free.

Challenge

Find a small space in your home that needs some healing. Release 27 things that no longer serve you and stop. Celebrate taking action without losing yourself in the big black hole.

Overcoming Resistance:
Four Days or Fifteen Minutes

For four days, I've watched patiently while my children's bedroom deteriorated into something resembling the tornado-ravaged communities you see on the news. Dishes began collecting on one table, the trash bin went from occupied to overwhelmed, and the backpacks and soccer equipment piled up in the middle of the room, making it look like a whole team lives in there. And while the two laundry baskets full of wrinkled-but-at-least-clean clothes tried hard to be the new closet, their dirty clothes piles (next to the baskets) expanded with each passing day.

Mothering has always had a distinct science experiment air about it for me. Now, eighteen years into it, I regularly opt to simply observe the creatures in their natural environment, watching to see what happens when I'm not directing their every move. I may "let things go" for a bit because I want to see what they choose without my intervention. Most importantly, I value the space that this gives them to explore and learn about themselves.

My own life experience has shown me that I am far more driven to take action because it makes me feel good to do so than I am to take action because the rules declare it so. It would be absolutely fabulous (at least in the short term) if I, somehow, created two children who were passionate about doing what I tell them to do, but... well, you know me, and seriously, what are the odds of that actually happening?

If I want them to be empowered to take action, then I need to allow them to learn that it feels better to take action, than it feels to be stuck in the over-whelm. Chasing them around with a bullwhip can't cultivate the healthy relationships they need to have with themselves in order to be functional adults.

(Yes, I just said that we can't be functional adults if we don't have healthy relationships with ourselves.

Resist as you might, but would you ever talk to your best friend the way you talk to yourself? Would you treat your partner's body the way you treat yours? Don't hate. You know it's true.)

I know that I can't force myself to act right because of some outside motivation; the desire has to come from within.

Finally, I mentioned that the room was getting sort of unwieldy and they agreed to tidy up. After school, as promised, they went straight to their room. When they came tearing down the stairs fifteen minutes later, declaring the room was clean, I couldn't help but laugh out loud at them. They'd spent four days of their lives living in a space that felt bad, allowing it to get worse, and losing oodles of precious mental and physical energy dreading the clean-up.

You had all that drama over fifteen minutes of action?

Yes, it seems they did, and guess what? We allow messes just like theirs to overwhelm our grown up lives, too. Confession: About once a week, I find myself at the intersection of *somebody-empty-the-dishwasher-because-dirty-dishes-are-taking-over-the*

-*kitchen* and *I-can-wash-them-and-dry-them-and-even-fold-them-but-dear-god-why-can't-I-get-this-laundry-put-away*. And there are millions of other things — pulling weeds, recycling, paying bills, eating well, working out, doing taxes, and what else? Oh yes, writing books. We feel resistance, just like the young people, and we let it keep us stuck!

If nothing else comes of you reading this thing, remember that it doesn't have to be this way.

Journaling to break through resistance

I've been journaling off and on since middle school, far more off than on until a few years ago. Looking back at the collective experience, I can identify three major perks of putting my pen, pencil, or Sharpie to paper. First, journaling is a fabulous way to explore my feelings. I've written my way through all manner of crises through the years, things that were all jumbled up in my head but seemed to make sense on paper (eventually).

Also, regular journaling is a fabulous way to document experiences that might otherwise slip right out of memory banks. For example, I have the most magical archives from my pregnancies and early motherhood. There are thoughts and experiences that otherwise would have long ago slipped from my mind.

The third thing is by far the most transformative, or at least it has been to me. It's the exposure of something of a dark side, that which I affectionately refer to as the nonsense factor. There is something undeniably concrete about writing down the things you say you are going to do and then following up in writing about how it's going from day to day. How many days can you write, "I didn't do it again today because blah, blah, blah…," before you begin to tire of your own excuses? It turns out, for me, not very long.

Ironically, the writing trick even worked with the writing. When I committed to Julia Cameron's "The Artist's Way" program, it meant writing morning pages every day. I wrote a couple of days, then something "came up" and I missed a day. Then, it was a few days, and before I knew it almost every entry started with, "Well, I haven't written in a while…" Blah. It only took a few weeks before I got sick of watching my hand write the excuses. I couldn't not notice how I wasn't doing what I said I was going to do, that which would result in something I claimed to want. It was shining a light on my promise, and it kept me from wandering off.

When we experience resistance, it's easy to move on to something else. There is always something willing to take my attention when the task at hand cultivates even the least bit of discomfort. Working out, cleaning the house, writing the book, and sometimes even answering emails. If you show me an activity that causes alarm, overwhelm, anxiety, sadness, really any uncomfortable emotion at all, I can show you something I'd be willing to push to the back burner.

If the task is something we already did well, then the change would already be made. If all of me wanted to lose this weight, it would already be off. If all of the parts of me wanted to be doing yoga every day when the sun comes up, I would already be doing it. The resistance comes from the conflict between the different parts of me, one that wants to do the new thing and one that thinks the old way is just fine (safe, easy, familiar, etc.)

Sometimes the "want to" part of me has to corner the "don't want to" part of me long enough to reason with it, "We want this... remember?" The thinking me really needs the feeling me to be willing to just stay put. Stay. My mind reassures my feelings, "We want to make the change. This is good. Stay with it. Don't run away because you feel a little (or a lot) alarmed. It's going to be okay."

This is how we face and move forward through resistance. We stay.

It turns out resistance is a big, huge, hairy deal when we're clearing clutter. It comes on early and strong. I heard people saying, "I'm making progress here but the paper... What's up with the paper? It seems like the more I do, the more I notice needs to be done." Ahhh, yes, this is the way of clutter clearing and especially with paper. The stuff in your physical environment is so deeply tied to your emotional state, your chaos, your pain, your whatever, your overwhelm, that there isn't a harder, more therapeutic task to be done in your home. This is you facing your stuff.

Count on this process to bring on the resistance.

So, let's say you have different types of paper spread in 12 piles in different areas of your house. You go to one and start to feel the resistance. It's inevitable. You're going to feel the resistance or the pile wouldn't be there to start with. And you're going to feel the desire to stand up and walk away, or perhaps run, because it is overwhelming. When we have that kind of dispersal of a project that's uncomfortable, it's easy to not make progress because we're bouncing around from one pile to the next.

There's something very empowering about putting everything in one spot — whether that's a bag or a box, or a stack of boxes, or a table where you just take all your piles and stack them side by side on a big table or on the floor. Move all of the piles of backlog paper to one place. It doesn't matter to me where you put it, but this is equivalent to telling this particular stuff, "You're not in charge here, I am. And before this is over, every single one of you will be where you belong or you'll be out of here."

To be clear (in case you haven't been reading long enough to figure this one out), if you cannot bring yourself to gather up all of those pieces of paper, then just work on them one at a time. But sit down, face one at a time, and do not surrender to the need to get up and wander off to something else. I've said it again and again: I don't care how we go, let's just go. And if you're struggling with anything on this path, do whatever you have to do… manipulate yourself in some way to make it so you can continue to move forward. Who am I to judge the method that works for you?

I suspect for most of us, gathering up all the papers is a power move. Because it's just impossible to be fooled by them if they're all in one place. So, gather them up. And then sit down and go to work. You're going to take breaks — for your job or sleep or food or whatever you need to do to take care of yourself — but then, you're going to come right back to work the next chance you get. By moving them to even a central location, you have moved them. You're beginning. You will be shifting the energy in your home and in your body. I honor the anxiety you might be experiencing, but take charge. It works.

It works because when the "want to" you backs the "don't want to" you into a corner for this respectful little chat, it's easier to stay put and dig in and get this done so you can move on with your life. This change will be behind you.

What was once incredibly stuck will be moving again, and you'll be back in the flow.

Challenge

Find a mess that you've been dreading — processing a stack of papers, emptying the refrigerator, putting away laundry, or clearing your inbox.

Now, set a timer for fifteen minutes, and go crazy.

Nine Clutter Clearing Tips for Paper Stashers

Here are the first nine clutter clearing tips for those who have bags, boxes, and stacks of paper stashed in the closets, spare bedrooms, dining rooms, and on counter tops all about this fine planet of ours.

1. Getting Things Done

Getting Things Done (GTD) is a book that will help you create a system for organizing your life that is both customizable and easy to implement. If you don't have a system that you use to manage your life (time, paper, contacts, projects, etc.), I recommend this one. It's been a miracle for me. You can get the book from any well-stocked book seller or borrow it from the library, and you can learn more about it and other GTD stuff online at www.davidco.com.

My approach is all about releasing what no longer serves you first, and then organizing and cleaning what remains is simple. If you're considering implementing the GTD system for paper (or any method for that matter), go ahead and journey with me through the releasing phase and you'll find implementing the new system to feel much more accessible. If you can't bear to wait to begin, GTD will guide you through its own releasing process. You may find the book doesn't address all of the emotional issues that create resistance. Come back to these chapters to find the support you need to get it done.

2. Centralize Your Paperwork

If the paper is spread out in different rooms, go ahead and collect it in one central location. This may feel overwhelming but I promise, it helps to keep you from well-intentioned wandering off. (This doesn't feel good so I'm going to check on those papers in the kitchen. Oh, that's hard too. I wonder how the papers in the dining room are doing... and on and on.)

Just make a massive pile, go to it, and dig in. First, release absolutely everything you can see no longer serves you. Shred what needs to be destroyed to meet your need for identity protection. If you have a fairly significant backlog, you'll find that most of the papers no longer serve you.

Next, you'll take action on the papers that require action. This may mean making calls, adding events to your calendar, and a slew of other activities. Don't panic. Just take action when it's possible and otherwise, collect these papers into a pile for you to tend as you move forward.

What remains is the paper you need to archive. You'll need a filing cabinet or some kind of system to hold the important papers. Most of us have a basic sense of how to do this step. Check out the GTD system if you don't.

When you need a break, walk away and then come back. Go to work and then come back. Eat dinner, play a game with the kids, kiss your valentine, and then find a few minutes to come back and do more. Keep coming back. It will work. Keep pushing that pile until it's gone. For some it might take a few hours, for others days, or even a few weeks. Don't worry, just dig in.

Oh, and if you don't know what to do with a particular piece of paper, set it aside and find someone to ask. Not knowing is a terrible excuse for staying stuck.

3. Financial Papers

Usually, as I've learned from my charming lot of paper stashers, the financial papers are mixed in with all of the other papers. That means you can't balance your checkbook, file your taxes, or make decisions about your retirement account. If that's your situation, consider starting a money box or bag to capture all of the financial papers as you proceed through the master pile. Some people even sort by the year, or type of financial papers, as they go through that first pass to make it easier to take action on them once the initial process is complete. Do whatever makes sense for you.

4. Other People's Papers

I've been so surprised to hear how many of my clients have papers in their stacks that belong to dead people. It's everything from financial papers to doctors visit notes, get well greetings to condolence cards, and from love notes to things like magazines and junk mail that would have been considered paper clutter even to the deceased.

Now, I know that it's hard to let go of things that belonged to our loved ones but let's think about these papers. Are they helping you remember what you long to remember about that person's life? When you look at those piles, are you consumed with fond memories? Usually not. These things aren't helping you remember them. You have memories, positive ones, and anything that doesn't support that isn't actually serving you. Letting go of that stuff isn't letting go of your loved one. In fact, it will free you up to remember them properly, in a way that honors the life you shared together. This stuff is in your way.

If there are papers that represent positive memories that you'd like to keep, go the distance to do it well. Make some sort of memory book, or even a simple file folder that you can retrieve from the filing cabinet every once in a while to refresh your memory. And if the papers represent action that needs to be taken, then be still, feel what needs to be felt, and do what needs to be done. Leaving things undone won't help you heal... it's okay to release them.

5. Pictures

Not everybody does this but I've learned that lots of people have pictures tucked away in their stacks of papers (digital clutter is a conversation for a different day). Release what no longer serves you and then gather the rest of the photos into a single location to deal with. When the paper backlog is eliminated, deal with your pictures as a single project.

6. Recipes

Oh how the recipes stack up around those with the best of culinary intentions! If you're going to go through the trouble of printing, copying, and tearing them out, at least use them. Make them accessible in a notebook, on index cards, or a folder in the filing cabinet. If you're feeling really savvy, go digital or virtual, but whatever you're going to do, do it. Don't let your affection for recipes take over your space!

7. Contact Information

Take all of the business cards, envelopes with your cousin's new mailing address, note cards, scraps of paper, websites, phone numbers, and whatever other paper you have there with contact information on it, and do something with them. It doesn't matter if you use a paper, electronic, or virtual system, commit to a system and use it to manage all of that information so you can release the paper.

Someone recently asked me what to do with referrals. Specifically, she was holding a piece of paper with the name of a doctor that a friend told her to see when she was ready for something that it wasn't time for yet. I suggested that she could do anything she wants to, as long as she does something with the paper so it's not in the pile and she can find it when she needs it. I suggested either emailing the info to herself with a description like "eye doctor referral from jane doe" (so she can search for it later), enter the details in her address book with the explanation in the 'notes' section, or create a file folder for them and put them away in the filing cabinet. If all of the things like this go in the same place, you'll know exactly where to go to find it when you need it.

8. Legal Papers

So far, all of the legal papers that my students have reported fall into three categories. They either need to take action on the papers (like divorce papers that need to be read to see if they are accurate before signing them), archive the papers (like birth certificates and such), or they simply need to be released or perhaps shredded and then released (like rough drafts of papers that were later finalized). If you have legal papers stacked up around you, do what needs to be done and free yourself from the daily reminders of the legal drama. At the very least, release what you can and then make a file for the rest and put them away in a cabinet. Leaving that stuff stacked up around you isn't helping you thrive. I promise.

9. Children's Papers

My kids bring home lots of paper. There are things that need action, like permission slips and order forms. There are art projects and completed assignments they bring home to share with me. There's a great deal of it and it's easy to be overwhelmed. It's important to release that which no longer serves you, and take the action that is needed. If there are events, put them on the calendar. If there are signatures, go ahead and commit and send the papers back.

As for the memories, each of my children have their own box in the storage room and we put our favorite things inside for safekeeping. I don't keep the fill-in-the-blank tests and such, as they don't actually capture much of the children's personalities or academic skills. I keep the papers and the stories they have to write. I keep the things that make me laugh or impress me. I keep things they are particularly proud of too. I've always told them that once they got too full, we'd go in and look for things that no longer serve us to release. They are both about to complete high school and the boxes are full. It's the boundary of a designated space that helps this potentially unwieldy category from taking over my space. We kept our best of the best within the space we had chosen to use to contain them.

What's in your piles?

For each paper, you have to first make a decision about what to do with it — release it, take action on it, or archive it. Then, you have to do with it whatever you decide. You have to either get it out of your house, take action (pay it/research it/call about it/do it/write about it/whatever), or find it a sensible home.

It's not always easy — especially when there are lots of papers — but it is that simple: decide on an action and take it. Decision making and action are the two things that don't happen when we're stuck. Then, we get overwhelmed by what's not happening so we accumulate more, make fewer decisions, and take less action. As that cycle continues, your hole gets deeper and deeper until you find yourself stuck. But you have the power to check back in.

Your sanity, your freedom, your life is waiting for you.

Challenge

Move all of the papers in your home to a single location (1 room or 1 table or 1 box... whatever it takes). Set a timer for 27 minutes. Then, find as many papers as you can to put in the recycle bin or bag during that 27 minutes. During this first pass, don't worry about things that need to be filed, require action, or belong to someone else. This is about releasing as many papers as you can in 27 minutes. Go!

Bonus Rounds: Take the paper challenge to a whole new level this weekend. If you're Unruly enough, that is. And yes, that's me taunting you. I want you to repeat, repeat, repeat, until there are no more first pass 'recycle' papers visible to you. (There will still be more recycle papers but all of the "low hanging fruit" will be gone, leaving you with the papers that have to be held, considered, and assigned to a category.

Ending the Paper Chase

My living room has thrown up paper. There is a volcano in the middle of a table and the entire surrounding area is finding some form of order. I can't get out until it's done, I guess.

- Shannon

Do you know that thing people say about it getting worse before it gets better? Well that certainly applies when clearing paper clutter. They have documentation of birth, death, and all that falls in the middle, and not only their own paper but the papers belonging to their loved ones too. Sometimes even paper belonging to those who've made transition into the next (please, oh please, let it be paperless) phase of life. We are covered up in paper.

Paper has to be one of the hardest kinds of clutter, at least in part, because it's so easy to hide. You know what I mean, right? People are coming over for book study, so you look around and discover that stack of papers on the counter (or dining room table or coffee table) and you shove the papers in a bag or box, then stash it in the office (or spare bedroom or coat closet or attic), vowing that you'll deal with those papers properly just as soon as your guests leave. You don't.

Then next month, when the book study returns, you put another bag with the first, and another... You know you're in trouble when you walk past that secret stash a few months (or years) later and think, for just a split second, that a well-placed house fire would give you the fresh start you really need. I get it. I really do but it's not good business to invite tragedy for dinner, so let's find another way for you to take back your life.

You are not alone, lots of people are covered up in paper. I think it's easy to be overwhelmed these days. Paper flows in at a Niagara-like volume. The pace we (attempt to) keep is certainly more intense than ever before. And then we have the cursed hows of getting rid of it. Paper certainly needs its own exit strategy. Where can we recycle? How long do we need to keep these things? To shred or not to shred? Now that is the question.

By the way, did anyone ever teach you how to manage your paper? If the people who raised you didn't include paper management on things-to-teach-the-wee-one game plan, then you may not actually know how to deal with all of the incoming papers. That's a very real challenge.

And if those people were afraid to release their papers, you probably are too. This is, of course, unless you are one of the rare apples that falls off the tree and rolls directly to the other end of the spectrum. In that case, you are probably reading this article just to see if it's really that important to keep things like birth certificates, journals, and your child's first painting. (It is, I promise.) Either way, the relationship that the people before us had with their stuff has a powerful influence on the relationship we have with ours.

We're really looking for something in the middle here, that elusive concept called *moderation*. I personally prefer the simplicity end of the moderation range, but to each their own.

Self-loathing is NOT a functional system for managing paper.

Most importantly, know that the shame and self-loathing do not help. They perpetuate the stuckness and if we want to free ourselves, we must find a way to let them go. If the problem is that you don't know how to do what needs to be done, recognize that and accept your reality for what it is. Admit you don't know how to do whatever it is, that you have a pretty big mess on your hands, and then get on with changing it.

It always comes back to decision-making, doesn't it?

Yes, a stack of papers (or any clutter for that matter) is quite simply something you haven't yet made a decision about. Unread magazines are something you haven't yet decided to read. Sure you think you made a decision to read it when you brought it into your house but really you just decided to buy, borrow, or steal it. Perhaps you even made a decision to think about reading it but you didn't decide to read it. I know this because if you had... those magazines would no longer be unread (or there would be time scheduled on your calendar to do so but almost nobody does that).

If you're unwilling to make time to read them, then you're unwilling to read them, so let them go. The same goes for the countless other "good ideas" you have stacked around you right now. It's art projects you meant to do, broken stuff you intended to fix, solicitations from organizations that you'd like to donate to, and invitations or advertisements for events that you think might be good to attend.

Commit. Either use it or let it go. (This is what my friends and clients sometimes call a "Christy – Love Her / Hate Her Moment.") "Want to" and "will" are two completely different things and when we cling to stuff that falls short of action we will actually take, we get stuck and life piles up around us. Yes, it is that simple.

You have to choose: yes or no. Are you in or are you out? Is this precious enough to take up space in your overwhelmed physical environment or is it not? Ask yourself, "Does this item serve me more than the space it occupies would serve me?" If not, release it.

It's time to take back your life.

Challenge

The paper clearing continues. Choose an amount of time you can commit to today and release as much as you possibly can. If this takes a few sessions, repeat it until it's done.

Considering
the True Value
of Papers

Strangely enough, the conversation about value started with a student who asked about business cards. Years ago she had a job that allowed her to meet a great many people and accumulate a great many business cards. She didn't actually know any of them but she was resisting letting them go. She said, "I feel like these are connections, potential connections, and while I've never used them, and I don't know what I'd use them for, I can't seem to make myself put them in the recycling pile."

Sometimes we cling to things that no longer serve us because we have a false understanding of their value.

If a business card is the only connection between us and another human being, it's probably not enough to consider us connected. If that encounter didn't result in something more substantial than a business card exchange, I'm not sure that these tokens of the encounter are actually worth keeping.

Again, this process is about releasing that which no longer serves us and a business card has a pretty specific range of possibility. It narrows with every day that passes without action. If you're going to be in touch, get in touch. If you're going to add some-one (with permission) to your professional newsletter list, add them. If you made a useful con-nection, do whatever you're going to do with it — reach out for lunch or coffee, schedule an appointment, or refer them to a friend in need. Add that person to your address book and let go of the paper.

Remember that releasing a business card that doesn't actually hold any value for you doesn't mean the other person is going to vanish from the face of the earth. It doesn't mean you didn't meet them. It doesn't even mean you didn't think they were cool, or nice, or pretty. It just means there is nothing else for you to do with their phone number and that means it doesn't actually serve you anymore. Its value has declined over time to the point that the space it occupies has more value than the business card. Let it go.

The same student possessed booklets, reports, and magazines from organizations that she had supported with her time and money in the past. Again, she was stuck because they felt so valuable — the work that went into them, the trees that it took to make them, and the information held within them.

Almost every paper stasher I've met so far has a profound respect for knowledge. We want to know all of that stuff. We want to be inspired. We care what these organizations have to say. We strive to learn and grow, to improve ourselves. It's all very noble but there is only so much time and so much space. Things start to pile up and soon we're stuck in the middle of a pile of good intentions.

I asked if she knew what all of that stuff really is, and she guessed, "Trash?" We laughed for a moment and then I explained that those things are actually promotional materials. Those companies and organizations don't send them to us, for us, they send them to us for them. They send them because it helps them stay connected to us.

Those things come so we will feel anchored to the organization because when they need us — our money, time, or connections — it helps if we feel the hook. And look around, it's working. We're hooked.

Here's the reality check: any information worth knowing will be available on their website or by contacting them. Unless we need to take a specific action on anything in those stacks of papers — at which point, I wholeheartedly encourage you to take it out right now and do whatever you need to do with it — let them go. Yes, thank those kind marketing experts for thinking of you, for sending you some inspiration or knowledge, or updates about how they spent your money, and let them go.

Again, it's a false perception of the value of those papers that keeps us hanging on to them. This is about pausing to recognize how these things can actually serve us. Yes, a recipe is valuable... if you're going to cook that meal. Yes, an article about employing social media to market your business can be valuable but only if you can actually find it, read it, decide if it resonates for you, and if so implement it. If not, let it go.

It doesn't matter how big or how small your pile is. When you consider the true value of your papers, a great many of them immediately become recyclable. Does this item serve me more than the space it occupies would serve me? Sure it's great but am I going to do something with this? If not... release, release, release.

Challenge

Paper. Paper. Paper. Keep pushing that paper. Release what no longer serves you, and do what needs to be done with the rest. Choose a number of minutes you can commit to each day to eliminating your paper backlog, something reasonable... and then do it.

Perspective Is Part of Life, And Part of Space Healing

This work has such tremendous healing potential that when a particular client is struggling to move forward, it's easy for me to get sucked into thinking it's all about me. Maybe my method is faulty, or I'm not paying enough attention. What if I'm not listening closely enough to deliver the just right message from the voices in my head? It's so tempting to think I'm "the problem," the barrier to their success, which is probably just a shallow, ego-driven attempt to take credit for the sluggish stories in order to take credit for "victories" too.

Don't get me wrong. I honor that I have a role in this, even that it is important to be the guide, teacher, storyteller, and divine comedian who shares these ideas and challenges old ways of being when I see them in the world. I found this river and I can guide you to it but drinking? Well, as the old saying goes, that's up to you. I can't force you to do anything that you're not ready to do.

But I'm surrounded by people who came to me to figure out how to do what they previously didn't want to do. It's a tricky job. There's so much contradiction in space healing. We want space for what's true to flow into our lives but we're afraid to release what resonated for us in the past. We want something brilliant and new but keep returning to our old ways of being. We want to remember the past but not so much it takes our future.

Oh my goodness, the past can be so deeply paralyzing. I don't think we made it through the first day of the first space healing workshop before dead people made their way into the conversation. And no matter how many times I teach it, death and dead people's belongings persist in the top three contributing "how I got here" factors.

As I look back, the stories seem nearly endless. One client had a basket full of expired medications from the hard, complicated years before her father died. Another woman's sanity all but collapsed under the weight of integrating her mother's belongings into her home as she transitioned to assisted living. When a child dies, it's like the world just stops spinning. We have been harnessed with the gifts, collections, and sometimes even entire houses that were chosen and coveted by people who are no longer with us. These dead people's things may or may not resonate as true for us but too often releasing them feels impossible.

Several older clients have revealed the intense motivation to heal their spaces, that they don't want their families to have to deal with it when they are gone. As we journey through the space healing process, every single person experiences grief for the loss of the years they didn't give themselves the gift of that freedom. There is something about facing our own mortality that helps us recognize that the stuff piled up around us isn't how we want our lives to be defined.

And then there was the woman who destroyed what I thought I knew about dead people's things:

"Hello, I just read about the 'Sick of Being Stuck September Challenge' and think it sounds like just what I need. I have Stage IV breast cancer, and whether I live or die, I need to get rid of all this stuff! I certainly don't want anyone else to have to deal with it... and if I live longer, think of how great it will be not to have it all around me. Of course, I'm worried that if I live, I will need the things I throw away — how ridiculous is that? Anyway, I would like to know where to sign up for the emails, and can I join mid-stream? Thanks."

- Meg

She danced in and out of my world for the next three years, tending to the chaos in her physical space at times that it energetically felt true for her. I learned that when you're dying a long, slow, painful death, there's a lot of paperwork — medical records, bills, research, end of life planning, and so much more. And when the fight to live gives way to the inevitability of dying, it's possible to live for years in the place between "there's still a dream alive in my heart" and not having enough energy, time, and money to give birth to that dream. She didn't know how to ask her community to help her create one last show when she might not even be able there to direct it. She didn't know if she could bear the possibility of, once she started, dying before the show ran.

When that incredible woman died last winter, she shattered my obsession with outcome. Whether we're talking about space healing or life itself, we must learn to covet the day to day process. This journey, one step at a time, is what makes our personal evolution possible. Destinations are inspiring but attempting to reach them in one leap is paralyzing. To truly, deeply, completely live in this moment, and this moment alone, is the only way to cultivate change.

Never mind the big picture. What needs to happen in this very moment? What action do you need to take right now? It's the only one we have at our disposal.

Pick up the phone to schedule the road test so your daughter can get her driver's license.

Stop everything and knit one square of that blanket that will probably take another year to finish.

Grab a bottle of red wine, two glasses, and the one that you love, and slip outside to watch the moon rise in the distance.

Leave those dishes in the sink and write the last, most impossible chapter that fits right in the middle of your first book.

Are You Stuck Because of Their Clutter?

Instead of ownership, when you pay for something, think of it as the cost of renting that item until it no longer serves you. Then, you can release it back into the river of stuff that flows throughout our society. We get hung up on the permanence of our relationship with the stuff and it leaves us stuck.

Have you ever bought a cool, shiny, new kitchen widget, used it three times, and then become bored with it? So, it sits there being not nearly as sexy as it was the day you met it in the store. Perhaps you have a pair of shoes that you just had to have, but they hurt your feet and are now collecting dust in the back of your closet. Or maybe you have an ever-expanding collection of movies, music, or books that, if you were inclined to notice how much you actually use them, you'd realize most of them won't be used again.

Why is it all still there? Most of the time, I've found that it's because we've committed to this stuff — or so it appears — with our hard-earned dollars. We brought it in the house and, even if we now recognize that we wouldn't bring it in again, we can't bring ourselves to take it out.

That is one of the most oppressive illusions I find in the minds of my students and clients as they work to reframe their relationship with stuff. Some people think it would be wasteful to give away (or sell at a second-hand price) something in which they "invested," which would no be longer true if we thought of our investment as paying a borrower's fee, as opposed to having made a life-long commitment.

Of course, there are others who believe the stuff they've accumulated somehow makes them better, more valuable. It's simply not true. Nothing outside of you can make you more of anything worth being.

So, while you're hoarding all of the things you've purchased but no longer use, the people in your community who desire those same exact things are driving to the store, purchasing new ones, and driving up the demand, so more of those things will be manufactured. But, what about stuff we might use again? Well, if you remember that the river of stuff flows both in and out of your life, then you're good. Maybe right now isn't the time for you to own that sewing machine after all. I mean sure, you bought it, but life changed and you never actually started using it. People ask me all the time how it's not irresponsible to release stuff that they may have to go buy again later.

Honestly, I don't believe that it is irresponsible. If you were sending it to the landfill, then yes, that would suck. But that's not what I'm suggesting. Let's use all of these magnificent resources we have through the Internet, nonprofits, and community programs to get that which no longer serves us into the hands of someone who can and will use it now.

When the time comes for that thing to flow back into your life, you can trust that you will have the resources to open the door and let it in. When there is something you want or need, remember to turn to all of the same fabulous sources you use when releasing your stuff. I'm not suggesting you buy at full price, release it when you don't use it for a while, then suffer later if you're not in a position to purchase it at full price again. There is a world here that's filled with everything we need. We just have to expand our understanding of the flow of stuff enough to live without fear, the fear that we won't be able to get what we want and need.

When the urge to possess an item passes, it is to make room in your life for something new. Why not just go with it?

Or is it that you think the urge hasn't actually passed? Well, I have news for you. It has. If the urge hadn't passed, you'd be using it. It doesn't mean you don't still think it's cool, or lovely, or inspiring. It means that, even with all of its awesomeness, this item no longer serves you. That means it's time for your stuff to go serve somebody else.

Before you throw this book at me, consider this: how much of that stuff have you actually gone back to after it sat for a few weeks or months or years? I know it occasionally happens, but let's be honest, these are truly rare experiences. Sometimes we do eventually get back to that instrument or creative outlet or appliance, but more often, we just keep it for a really, really, really long time, and then, we release it anyway. It might be because of a move or perhaps it will be taken from us by a tornado or something a little less dramatic. We cling until we are pushed, and then we let it go.

Why not let it go now? Why keep sharing your space with stuff that somebody else needs?

The people who come to my classes truly want the freedom that comes from releasing that which no longer serves them, but we've all been taught to cling. We are groomed to believe this story about the permanence of stuff, but what if we just decided it wasn't so? What if we shifted our relationship with stuff, and were able to make space in our lives for what we really want?

Seriously, let's have the courage to release these things back into the river of stuff that flows through our society. You can sell it, donate it, recycle it, or just give it away. My clients have gotten downright crafty with their releasing lately. One young woman keeps carrying loads of stuff out to the curb with a "Free" sign; and while she does more releasing inside, there's a serious celebration underway at the street as people find things they want and need. Others are donating treasures to museums, neighbors, or family members for whom these items now feel true. There are shelters that need donations and collectors who are looking for their next great thing. The options are really endless.

How are your partners, children, and roommates (or whomever you live with) going to feel about this? Well, you're probably going to be the trailblazer in this situation. They were raised in the same society that you were and are probably clinging to the stuff that no longer serves them, too. You're going to be all pumped up with the possibility of freeing yourself from yesterday's inventory, and welcoming into your life the space, time, energy, and cash that comes from this experience. But be prepared… they may not share your enthusiasm.

Don't worry. This happens all the time. In fact, my classes are full of people who are the first in their house, family, and circle of friends to have made the switch to this more simple, community-conscious way of living. The good news is that you don't have to convince them to get on board. (Trust me, you don't want to be in charge of that.)

For now, just focus on releasing the stuff that no longer serves you. The freedom you are cultivating is undeniably attractive and the people around you will want to know what's gotten into you. Your shift will cause other shifts. That is always the case. And if I'm wrong, which I've never been on this one before, you can always just tell them to take it up with me!

I share my closet with my husband, who could also stand to shed a few items… if I set some of his things out for consideration, and he is up for relinquishing them, can I count these as part of the 27?

The "other people's clutter" conversation started on the very first day of the very first day of the very first workshop I ever offered around space healing. The challenge was quite simple: go to your closet and find 27 things that no longer serve you. Donate them, consign them, whatever, but do it today. One woman's response, above, made me laugh out loud. On one hand, I totally understand that feeling: "Sure, I've got stuff to let go of but what about the rest of the people who live here? What about his/her /their stuff?" On the other hand, that's the kind of thinking that keeps us stuck.

We are the only people we can control.

This can be difficult because... well, we aren't on this planet alone. Most of us share our space with others — parents, children, partners, and roommates. We share our work spaces with co-workers, bosses, and employees. Even our home spaces bump against our neighbors' spaces. It's almost impossible to keep other people's stuff from showing up on our radar when we consider the relationships.

The power position, of course, is remembering that your space healing journey is about you. (There is more to be said about those for whom we are responsible, like our children, but that's a conversation for a second book.) Clear 27 of your own things and then encourage your partner to do the same. Let's face it, if you find yourself holding this book, you probably won't have any trouble culling 27 items to release from your closet.

Clearly, I can't force her, or you for that matter, to get rid of stuff. You're doing this so you can take back your life. And it's not going to help your stuck-ness to get rid of other people's stuff. I know this to be true, not because I'm a super-savvy organizational goddess but because I live with people, too!

Before I go putting my nose into their business, do I have anything that no longer serves me hanging around? Do I have clutter to clear? The answer is always, always, always yes. And once I start tending my own things, my attitude immediately improves.

Challenging
Convenience Clutter

Have you ever noticed the blurry line between convenience and clutter?

I first discovered the concept of Convenience Clutter in my bathroom. The cough medicine which usually resides in the bottom drawer was sitting out on the counter because I was sick and had been taking it a few times a day. It was convenient to have it there because I didn't have to get it out and put it away every four to six hours. As I started to feel better, I used it less frequently and for the final two days I just took it before I went to bed at night. A few more days passed and I was well enough to not think about cough medicine.

A week later, I realized that the cough medicine was still on the bathroom counter. It was as if it had become a permanent fixture there, like the cup that holds toothbrushes or the soap dish. I saw it, realized it hadn't been used in a while, and put it away.

I've been sort of obsessed with identifying, under-standing, and releasing different types of clutter lately and this one really got my attention. I couldn't help but notice that with the cough medicine what was just convenient a week ago had shifted into something different. What was under one set of circumstances very helpful became clutter when the situation changed.

I've decided that at least part of the problem is the speed with which I'm passing through life. When I shop at my preferred pace — calm, centered, engaged in one activity at a time — I wait for the receipt, fold it up, and slip it into my wallet. When I high-speed shop, I shove my wallet into my purse as soon as I've swiped the debit card and the receipt gets dropped as an afterthought into my purse or the bag as I race to the next thing.

It takes just a few errands at this pace and suddenly I can't see my keys in my junked up purse, so I pull the handful of papers out and leave them on my desk before dashing out the door again. And then the mail comes and I add it to the desk and then the permission slips and order forms from my children's school come in. It just takes two or three days of high-speed Christy before I take my laptop to the couch to write because I can't deal with the papers on my desk.

You might have already seen this coming but debit card receipts piled up on the desk, while I'm off doing whatever else, means that the checkbook registers aren't being maintained. Without some attention, that can only go a couple of ways. I will either accidentally spend money I don't have, or keep putting off important things like paying bills because I don't know how much money I have. Frankly, both of those options suck.

I've worked hard not to be that girl... and when I go too fast, it's convenient to take short cuts, and before long life gets sort of junked up.

I have a thing where every pair of shoes wants to gather by the doors so they'll be ready when I need them again. I don't mind running upstairs to get my hiking boots out of the closet before I head to the woods but when I come home, I have all manner of resistance to putting them away.

It'll be so convenient to have the boots by the door when I want to go to the woods again tomorrow. But in the spirit of full disclosure, I almost never go to the woods tomorrow. So for days those hiking boots sit there waiting to go to the woods, I see them about 30 times a day and think, "Oh, I'm not hiking," and often other less-supportive thoughts.

And if we were only talking about one pair of hiking boots, it wouldn't be a big deal but we're not. I have a pair of sandals I sometimes slip on to go fetch the mail or the children, or to grab something out of the shed. I have the shoes I wear every day and a dressier version of that shoe for when they are appropriate. Plus, I have a pair of super sexy, red patent-leather high heeled shoes that I wear when I go out.

Plus, I share that space by the front door with other people. Next thing you know, there are a dozen pairs of shoes by the front door. Yes, any single pair of them is convenient to slip into but a bunch of anything piled up anywhere in our humble home is enough to drive me out of my mind.

Convenience Clutter is the stack of donation requests piled up on the counter and the medicines we plan to take again tomorrow. There are jackets and dog leashes, and the broom that don't make it back to the utility room before something else needs to be swept up.

No single thing is a crisis but together it completely overwhelms.

We have very little storage here, so the camping stuff and the Christmas decorations are in the basement. I loathe carrying either of those sets of things back up there, but the alternative is to keep the tent pitched out back with all of our gear set up inside. It doesn't make sense. Neither does keeping our Christmas decorations out all year round, right? It doesn't make sense.

It feels like a matter of balance. We have to balance time, extra seconds here and there, with the visual simplicity of having those things put away between uses. I invest an extra 60 seconds in putting the hiking boots back in my closet, and it keeps me from having to look at them over again and again for days, even weeks, between my trips to the woods.

To keep from being overwhelmed, I take the shoes back to the closet until I need them again. I return the book to the book case until I need it again. I file the papers. I put the pants I'm going to wear again back in the closet instead of at the foot of the bed. I get out the hairdryer and put it back every single day because it saves me and the rest of the family from having to look at it the rest of the time.

It's the same with all of this stuff.

If everything we might need stays out all of the time, then it is going to overwhelm. We will get stuck. We can't decide which thing to do first, and we feel like we're never finished.

To keep from having space completely overwhelmed, invest the energy it takes to stay on the sanity-supporting side of that line between convenience and clutter.

Challenge

Survey your environment. Can you find any convenience clutter? Where does it really live? If you're unwilling to have it "put away," can you give it a new home? Somewhere that feels more true, convenient without feeling cluttered?

Is Your Kitchen
Making You Fat?

Relationships. Relationships. Relationships.

It doesn't matter what my clients bring to the table, our work together always seems to come back to relationships. It may be our relationships with others that need to be tended — partners and old flames, children and parents, bosses and clients. More often, buried below those relationships, we find an even more important one to tend; our relationship with self. It is most often revealed in our dance with money, food, creativity, and spirit, but that song plays out in a million different ways between the first day and the last day of every single one of our lives.

Naturally, all of these relationships manifest in our physical space, in the places we call home. The relationship between each of us and our space is a profoundly reciprocal one. We make our environment and it makes us right back. We cultivate around us a life that reflects what lives within us, and then our environment perpetuates much, much more of the same.

This is, of course, the good news... and the bad.

Pluck twenty morbidly obese people out of their homes and place them on a ranch where meals are healthy, gym time is abundant, and every person in sight is singularly focused on improving health and and you've got yourself a recipe for remarkable weight loss success (and a wildly popular TV show). I suppose that's more than good news for those individuals, it's great! We are talking about an epic opportunity, the invitation to change your life by going to live in a radically supportive environment like that.

We make our environment and it makes us right back.

You may be living with an oven that's warmed a thousand pizzas in its lifetime, plus a volume of cookies, muffins, and other doughy goodness that are probably best left alone. It might be that the exact pantry you have to eat out of tomorrow hosted an incalculable number of calorically-intense, yet absolutely nutritionally-void processed and pre-packaged foods for years leading up to this. And the handle on that fridge door may be the very same one that you pull day after day to access a rather enviable inventory of meats and cheeses, dressings and juices.

You may be living in the place you created when you were living in a way that you no longer want to live.

Every kitchen tells of a story about the way its residents use it. The stains on the coffee maker whisper about exhaustion and headaches, while the blackened pizza stone reveals overwhelm and perhaps even guilt. Worn metal reflects the image of a loving woman searching for numbness and security by sweetening the lives of others. The crumbs piled up within the toaster mean that the children caught the bus with food in their bellies but perhaps not the nutrition they needed. The drawers boldly designated as home for all "Fresh

Foods," tell about hope and promise followed by sameness and betrayal, when everything in them turns to mush.

We make our environment and it makes us right back. It's like giving someone a shovel, just to have them give it back, again and again until there's a hole so deep that you can't find your way out.

Let's say you moved out and someone else moved in and let's imagine that it's a woman with a far more functional relationship with food. Her new kitchen would, without question, rise to the occasion. She would come into your old environment, the one that failed to support every fresh start you attempted to make, and she would make it into her environment. And guess what? Yes, it would make her right back. That very same pantry and fridge would allow her to create meals and snacks that cultivate life, energy, joy, and physical health; the very same things you never could find in there.

What would it take for you to give yourself that same fresh start? Are you willing to clear those cabinets of all that perpetuates the myth that this version of you is the best one you'll ever get to be? If you're ready to make a change, why not just let all of that crap go? Give yourself a fresh start, the most generous gift of a sparkly clean slate. Let go of every single thing that no longer serves you. Why not? The only thing you have to lose is extra pounds.

Your environment will make or break you. Period. It's that big of a deal. If there are changes that you're trying to make — health related or otherwise — look around you. Is your physical environment supporting the person you were five minutes ago or the person you want to be? If you're ready to make a change, start there. Start this healing with the place you call home.

As always, if you can make this change on your own, GO FOR IT! Do it. Seriously, I'd love nothing more than to hear that you got it done after reading this book. If, however, you find yourself stuck and unable to cultivate the change you desire, please know that many people — yes, including me — need more during times like these. There is nothing wrong with giving yourself the gift of support. Remember: Do something. Do anything. Do whatever you can to not be in this same exact spot tomorrow.

And, the more radical action you choose, the better!

Challenge

Go into the kitchen and find 27 things that are not
supporting your health goals and let them go.

"Just In Case" Clutter

Does this item serve me more than the space it occupies would serve me? We always start with that question but if that's not enough, ask more! What would I do if I 'needed' this and didn't have it? Could I get by without it? Could I borrow it? Can I trust myself to gain access to this thing when the need arises? What will be the consequence if I need it and can't substitute, borrow, or buy it?

Perhaps most importantly, what am I afraid will happen if I don't have this?

Just last week, this one helped me with a decision. I've had two baking stones — one round pizza stone and one rectangle stone, both incredibly well seasoned, as I've had them for years. Having two meant that I was constantly shuffling around when I need to use the oven, which had begun to drive me crazy. I was trying to decide if I could let one go. That means that yes, I had determined that the space was more important than two stones.

I decided one had to go but which one? I went back and forth and back and forth. And then, I asked what I would do if I needed the round one and didn't have it. There are things (like pizza!) that won't fit on the rectangle one and what would I do if I needed it and didn't have it. I didn't know! It would have been pretty inconvenient, probably on a weekly basis, to be without the round one. When I applied this inquiry to the rectangle stone, I realized that I do have (and plan to keep) one metal cookie sheet in the drawer under the oven. So if I didn't have the rectangle stone and I needed something with a lip (which the round pizza stone doesn't have), I would just substitute the metal pan.

Can you get by without it? How big of a deal would it be if you couldn't substitute or borrow, and you had to possess another one? What if it was next month, would it be terribly inconvenient? What about 1 year? What about 5 years?

Challenge

Get out a "Just In Case" bag/box/etc. Walk around and look for anything that's in your space, not because you love or use it, but just in case you need it in the future. Remember the magic question is, "Does this thing serve me more than the space it occupies would serve me?" If you're still unsure, ask more questions.

What In The World Is Wannabe Clutter?

I want to be the kind of woman who hems too-long curtains and pants. Since I am only 5'2 and our cat sheds on everything he can reach, this desire is not as romantically domestic as it may sound. This is about being functional, too. I want to make pillows that match the new couch. I want to make gifts with nothing but a trip to the fabric store and the sweat of my brow. Okay, that one was a little dramatic but you get what I'm trying to tell you. I want to be the kind of woman who sews.

I always wanted to be this kind of woman. I even paid $172.50 for a sewing machine on December 17,

1996. I can tell you that because I am actually the kind of woman who tapes her receipts inside the owner's manual and then files them in an expandable file folder in the filing cabinet. Don't laugh, we all have our issues. Okay, go ahead and laugh.

You and I both know that getting you to laugh about my clutter is one of the most effective means by which I taunt you into considering your own relationship with stuff.

A few months into sewing machine ownership, I made a single, square curtain to hide an ugly cabinet under the sink in a half bath. I was filled to capacity with my first child and in hindsight, I credit some sort of nesting instinct for the incident. It was the most crooked little curtain I'd ever seen but I made it and I was excited about it. Mostly, I was excited about not seeing the ugly cabinet, but whatever.

I have no recollection of sewing anything else with that machine. Nothing. Not one other item or repair did I produce with that machine. Oh, and that baby I was brewing the last time I used it is now a legal adult. I wish I was kidding. I am decidedly not, by any visible measure, the kind of woman who hems too-long curtains and pants.

My sewing machine is clutter.

It's not junk. It's a fine little machine. It will do whatever I might need it to do… except turn me into the kind of woman who hems curtains and pants.

And it's not that I'm not capable of being that woman. For the most part, I've been able to do whatever I wanted to do. It's a matter of choosing to invest the resources to make it so. I haven't done it and since that machine sits there in the closet, do you know what other clutter I just realized I have? I have a stack of pants that cannot be worn because they are too long.

I haven't hemmed them because I can't. I don't know how. But, I also haven't taken them to be hemmed because I am haunted by that sewing machine tucked away in the back corner of the closet. If I didn't have the machine (because I want to be that woman who…), then those pants would have long ago been taken down the street to the nice lady who will make them fit for a few dollars each.

Seriously. What the heck?

So today, I'm fixing this. I'm releasing my sewing machine, and my want to be the kind of woman who sews. If I can do it with a needle and thread, then I will. If not, I will either pass on the project or pants, or I will pay a woman who sews to sew it for me. And if someday in the future the want to be the kind of woman who sews flairs up again, I choose to trust that the universe will provide for me another fine, fine machine.

Challenge

Find (at least) 27 pieces of wannabe clutter. Then, trash the trash and get creative about how to gift the creative treasures (think schools, scouts, community centers, other artists, etc.). Consider these things:

- Ideas that once turned you on but — if you're honest with yourself — no longer excite you (making room for ideas that will get you fired up)

- Art that no longer inspires you

- Supplies/materials that no longer fit your vision

- Incomplete projects

- Instructions for projects you "should" do (but aren't going to)

- Broken stuff you're unwilling to fix today

- Unclean materials that you're unwilling to clean today

Celebration
and Other Essential Tools

"It seems like every single one of the women in my circle of friends has a thing they want to do, or a big change they want to make but we're all just stuck. Nobody is moving forward on anything."

This is how we started a group call one morning and I thought, "Oh, wow, here we go!" Before I could even get the recording turned on, she offered an explanation for why she signed up. She divorced a few years ago, went back to school, and is now working her new field and raising her kids. She loves her much smaller house and lots of things are really great but she just feels stuck.

Her big thing is the paper. Another student tells us that it's the basement packed to the brim with boxes filled with all manner of assorted whatnot that didn't get tended in a recent move. She can't bring herself to open even one box. Another student has a series of tiny little spaces — a room at home (sharing the rest of the space with roommates), a car, and a cubicle at the office. It's a professional shift that she is here to cultivate.

I continue to marvel at the wild varieties of people and issues that pop up in my world, which is nothing compared to the similarities we're uncovering. This experience is a remarkable one. We're all just the same.

We get stuck for the same reasons — people die, marriages end, kids come into our lives or grow up, or perhaps it's a health crisis. We have dreams for something new but can't figure out how to fit it into our lives. We set goals but the sameness keeps pulling us back into the old ways of being. And after we've outgrown parts of our lives, sometimes we stay put and the stuff stacking up around us gets too sticky to make a move.

When we are mocked for not having a cool enough wardrobe when we are little, we often become obsessed with clothes that will keep us from feeling that way ever again. Of course, we can't actually fix an inside problem by piling things on externally but we try.

Eventually, the stuff becomes as oppressive as the original bully.

We all react to our old wounds in ways that show up in our space. We are so hard on ourselves. Painfully hard. Ironically, or perhaps tragically, it doesn't help. Over and over again — in these group calls and also in my own head — I listen to people beating themselves up about whatever isn't yet complete or perfect.

As you know, my approach is anchored on releasing the excess first, which makes organizing and cleaning become possible. In the workshops, we always begin with a short period of small, daily clutter clearing challenges. The first day, for example, I challenge them to remove and release 27 things that no longer serve them from their bedroom closet. Inevitably they experience a big rush of excitement when they do the simple task, followed by an almost immediate crash.

It's the realization that there is still so much still to be done clouding the celebration. It is a seriously oppressive pattern. Just like wallowing in yesterday, the forward-thinking hysteria won't help anyone with anything, except maybe inviting more suffering, and who needs more of that?

We have to remember to stay in this moment. It took time to get here and we all know that it's going to take time to get back in balance. We've heard that a million times, whether it's about extra weight or clutter or healing from an injury. What we don't talk about is how devastating it is to beat ourselves up. If something major happens in your life — a loss or trauma, in particular — and you stop tending your space for a while, things will get backed up. If you beat yourself up about it, it won't ever get better. It can't.

We have to learn what we can from the past and then have the courage to let it go. Clinging to what was true yesterday cannot support us tomorrow. We have to learn to live now, in this moment.

Learning to celebrate what is real right now is essential to leaving the past behind without allowing what lies ahead to move right in and rain on the parade.

Every moment that you're moving forward is worth celebrating. And no, it doesn't matter how small the step is that you're taking. Every little thing you let go of — physically, emotionally, or mentally — puts you back in the driver's seat of your life. Each intentional action opens you up to the possibility of the next one.

When you walk 5 minutes for the first time, it makes it easier to do it again. When you clear out one drawer, it makes it possible to do the next one. When you ask for what you need in a situation when it's really, really difficult to do so, the next time it will be easier. And every single time, stop and celebrate because you have just taken action. This action will cultivate the change you desire.

That step means that you won't ever again have to stand in the spot you were in yesterday. That step is everything when your intention is to change your life. That step is worth celebrating. YOU are worth celebrating.

Here are a few other things that can dramatically improve your space healing experience:

1. *Music.* I don't know the science behind it but everything is better to a beat. At my house,

what's good enough for a party is good enough for putting away laundry. And the more resistance I'm feeling to the task, the louder the music has to be to get me moving.

2. *Flowers.* Perhaps it's a little like giving myself a reward for something I haven't done yet, but bringing flowers into the space I need to work in certainly lifts my mood. Also, tending my inside plants will usually get me moving again. If I'm stuck and dusting isn't sexy enough to get me off the couch, then watering the plants usually inspires enough to at least get me vertical.

3. *Company.* When I was a kid, I figured out that cleaning up with a friend was usually more fun than doing it alone. The same is true for me today. While it is certainly nice to have had help cleaning up after a sleep-over when I was young or a play date when I had them for my children, or after a dinner party like I might have today, I find that it is actually the company that makes it much better for me.

This might mean that your friend comes to help you clean one day and the next time you go help your friend, or it might just mean that you call up a friend to chat while you're doing some of the mindless activities. As long as you remember to be productive, a helper can make the time pass more quickly, help keep you focused, and assist you with the decision making process (especially around what can be released).

4. *Game plan.* I work with all of my new students to craft a strategy that's customized to their space, a game plan to help them. It's so easy to wander off when you're doing something that's hard, so write a list of what you intend to do and keep checking back in with it to make sure you stay on track.

5. *Reality Check.* Whether you're taking on the nightmare beneath and behind the washing machine and dryer, as I did this week, or tackling the piles of paper between you and your dining room table, take pictures before you begin. Picture-taking serves many purposes, not the least of which is drawing a metaphorical line in the sand. This is you saying, "Hey, it's about to be over between me and you. Any final words?"

It also allows you to truly see what's happening there. Sometimes that is seeing stuff that you've overlooked for a long time, and other times, you'll see that the situation is not as bad as it *feels*. Either way, it always helps. And when you are finished, you can look back at the pictures and celebrate how strong and smart and accomplished you are!

6. *Accountability.* This is one of the strongest benefits of my workshops, but even if you're not in one, you will absolutely benefit from creating an accountability system for yourself. Tell someone your intention for the day, then report back with your progress as the day passes. Post your intention on Facebook, Twitter, or wherever else you are connected to other human beings. If you journal, write it there, or wherever else you will see it to remind you about the commitment you made to yourself.

7. *Celebration.* You already know about this one, right? If you feel resistance to an activity, then put a carrot on the end of a stick and taunt yourself into taking action. *After I clear off the kitchen counter, I'm going to go to the park for a nice hike. Once this bathroom is clean, I'm taking a hot bath!* I always ask my intro students to decide how they will celebrate

when they reach their program goals. It feels good to party; go ahead and plan yours!

Whether you're looking at one huge project or a million little ones, it's important to remember... *you can do this.*

Yes, I'm sure.

Challenge

Release something big. I don't mean necessarily physically to move big, like a couch or a car. I'm talking about something that's big emotionally, or that you have to go an extra mile to find a good home for. Do something that once it's done, you'll want to celebrate. Then go celebrate. Yes, I'm serious.

Empty House:
Made for TV Clutter Clearing

I just had an idea for my own television series. It would be the ultimate clutter clearing/take back your life adventure. Each episode would begin with my search for a person or family who will say yes to each of the following questions:

- Are you stuck?

- Are you sick of it?

- Do you believe that releasing that which no longer serves you from your physical environment will free you to make the changes you desire, or are you at least willing to suspend any disbelief to try a different approach to change?

I would take the person or family out to a nice, long dinner where I (and the viewers) would begin to learn about what has them stuck. We would talk about their home and their stuff and what it would take for them to truly enjoy life again. Then we'd have a nice night of sleep, followed by a day of more intense coaching.

I would ask them to envision their home restored to an ideal state. We would mentally walk through the spaces together, crafting a vision, conceiving of new ways to find and keep balance in the stuff-to-space ratio. We would talk about company and hobbies and work and play, and how that home could host more health (physical, mental, emotional, relational, financial, spiritual, etc.). We would talk about storage and cleaning and the different types of areas necessary to accommodate the life that they desire, the life that currently feels out of reach.

Meanwhile, back at the ranch, a wildly efficient crew would be carrying every single thing these nice people own out onto the front lawn (or other workable space). All of their possessions would be grouped by the room they came out of and would be displayed on tables and shelves and in bins. The house would be cleaned from top to bottom, and just for fun, let's pretend I even have a small budget to spend on repairs and such.

With the home restored to "blank canvas" state, I would guide them (blindfolded, of course) right through the middle of the yard which is full to the brim with their every possession, and into the middle of their Empty House. I would ask them how they are feeling, invite them to remove the blindfolds, cut to a commercial break, and then return to watch them process the shock that my crew did not swoop in and "fix" this for them.

I would tell them, "It's not possible for me to give you the dream but we all came here to support you in giving yourself the dream." And then, we'd walk together back outside to face their stuff because as we all know, that stuff is where the stuckness lives. They will be genuinely shocked at the amount of stuff they own, disoriented probably, and we will begin the journey back to sanity by "auditioning" every single item that they own.

Pausing to consider each thing is still the only way to decide what stays. They would ask again and again, "Does this item serve me more than the space that it occupies would serve me?" That's how we decide if our things are worthy of going back into the sacred space, to be a part of the new dream. Yes, I said every single item must be auditioned.

What doesn't go back in would, of course, be released in the most earth-friendly way possible. We would donate, repurpose, recycle. We might have a yard sale to turn some of the stuff that no longer serves them into cash. Basically, I always want people to release that which no longer serves them as responsibly as they possibly can.

- This is the wedding dress... it's been four years since I said, "Never again," and asked him to leave.

- These are the cards my dad received when my mother passed away. And somewhere here we'll find the cards from when daddy died.

- I know it seems like a lot of clothes, but my weight fluctuates so much that I hate to let go of those. I might need them again.

That's what we'd do. That's my dreamy show idea. One home at a time, we'd show those who are sick of being stuck how to free themselves. We would dig around in the stories just long enough to find the hooks so that they can release that which no longer serves them back into circulation, allowing those items to serve someone new.

This show would be about recreating the vision, the dream of their lives, that so often slips away in the old, untended wounds and habits learned from the generation before... and then moving into alignment with that vision. Life happens. We get stuck. What matters is that we find a way to let go of the pain and shame, so we can take back our lives.

To be clear, I'm not talking about another show for hoarders, although that work inspires me deeply (and horrifies me sometimes, too). And it's not even a show for people who want their house restored and their hearts healed, like all of the goodness we enjoy on HGTV. I'm more of a normative chaos kind of guide, if there is such a thing. I want to work with people whose lives are stuck; people who are reasonably functional but who are not living the dream.

I want the dream.

You know what I'm talking about, right? These are people living like lots of us are living — too tired to write the book, too worried to invest in themselves, too uncertain to try to be the person they dreamed of being when they were little. I want to support people who long to live more simply, so that they may have time for love and health and dancing. We must make more time for dancing.

It's a positively dreamy gig to me. I don't know how anybody ever just "gets a show," but if anyone ever asks, I will be ready. And in the meantime, I've just written a story about a pretend show that tells you exactly what you need to do to get yourself unstuck. Craft a vision, hold auditions, and get every single thing that no longer serves you out of your sacred space. Your life is waiting to be lived. Enough is enough. Get to it!

Challenge

Release 27 things that you know wouldn't make it back in the house if I came with my pretend crew and emptied the contents of your house onto the front lawn.

Making Space for What We Want

There's a healer with a magical touch, who dreams of doing what she was created to do but the thing she does for money leaves her lost, separated from her truth. Another wild one longs for love but holds back because giving her heart means opening her home, and it's haunted by piles of who she used to be. And there is the one who aches to run and dance and twist her body in soulful ways who hasn't even a few hours each week to cultivate the strength she knows belongs to her.

Something must be terribly out of alignment when we — you and me — haven't the time and energy and money (or whatever other obstacle we find between us and ourselves) to be who we were born to be.

We must make space in our lives for what we desire.

If we want to grow something new in the natural world, everyone knows to begin by making a space for the new thing to grow. We get on our hands and knees and prepare the landscape — the garden, flowerbed, or pot of soil. We release the grass, weeds, or remains of last years' growth that occupy that space, so that new life can have the opportunity to thrive.

You and I are part of the natural world, why would the principles that govern our lives be any different than what thrives in the wild? It isn't. In many ways, our lives and wildlife are the same.

What is it that you want to grow in the gardens of your life? What are the seeds in your heart that your soul pines for? Look within for your answers and then, look around you. Do you have the space — the time, energy, attention, and money — to plant and nurture what you've just called into your experience? Or perhaps you've resisted asking for fear that there isn't a way?

What about your physical space, is there room for you in your life? I've heard a handful of stories in the last five years about people who, with the intention of inviting love, made space for a future partner in their home by releasing that which no longer served them. They emptied half of the bedroom closet, dresser, bathroom drawers, and kitchen cabinets. One woman even left one side of the two car garage open for the one she was open to.

That is a bold statement of intention, isn't it? They might as well scream to the universe, "Hey YOU! Can you see me? I am ready for love!" It takes a great deal of courage to be willing to see emptiness in your home, to be reminded that what's coming hasn't yet arrived. I can't help but think that kind of openness, that willingness to feel what is in order to prepare for what's next, is incredibly attractive.

I love the magic — at least it feels like magic — when I'm able to trust and everything just falls in line.

To be honest, it's rarely what I thought would happen or even what I said I wanted to happen. But still, it's undeniable that when I am open, what I want and need flows into my life.

When I finally let go of those too-tight blue jeans, a friend gifted me three bags of the most beautiful, stylish, comfortable clothes that fit me like a glove, including four pair of perfect blue jeans. And I love that every single time I have the courage to release a cool idea because it wasn't cool enough to resonate with anyone else, a more magnificent, fabulously-attractive idea comes through and expands me and my business to a whole new level of success.

Yes, that's where we are. You're reading this book because I was willing to release the last good idea, which made room for the whole space healing adventure to flow in. It happens all the time to people all over the world. We just have to have the courage to make ourselves available.

We must make space in our lives for what we desire.

So, what is that thing that you want to cultivate in your life? If it's love, is there space in your schedule and your closet for that special someone? Do you have time to get to the gym for workouts, or the space in your kitchen to make food that supports the body you're creating? Are you making yourself available to study your dreams, to pursue your passions, to seek mastery in your field? Is there room in your house for the drop cloth and easel if painting makes your heart sing?

It's time to take back our lives, to make ourselves available for the brilliant and beautiful experiences that await us. Let's release that which no longer serves us and free ourselves from the past, from that which has us stuck. Why not give ourselves the same opportunity we've been giving our parents and children, bosses and lovers, our friends and everyone else we've supported along the way?

I can't say for sure how it works but I know that it is true. If you create the space, plant the seed, tend it properly, the beautiful life that belongs to you will come for you. It's as if everything simply begins to realign. It's not always easy but it is simple, and now is the time.

Your life is waiting for you.

Challenge

It's time to build your clutter courage. Make a physical space for something you want but don't have yet. That might mean releasing the deep fryer to make space for a fancy blender that you can use to make smoothies and soups that will promote health. It might mean releasing non-fitting clothes to make space for clothes that will allow you to feel strong, confident, and beautiful at whatever size you are today. Or maybe you'll release the tools and remnants from an old creative passion to make space for your new one. Listen to your heart.

Move Pebbles, Not Mountains

I've been trying to move mountains for 20 years and frankly, I'm tired. Aren't you tired, too?

There are a million ways to travel from the beginning to the end of your life. Some trips are longer than others, some paths are more intense. It seems to me that of all of the lives that we could possibly experience, there is one path for each of us that is the most true. There is a specific path, a certain series of conditions and decisions and circumstances, that will allows us to cultivate our best possible lives.

I can now see that as far as my health goes, I missed a turn, or a series of turns, somewhere along the way. This body, my body today, and my true body (me without the consequences of not eating well, using food to medicate, and living a relatively sedentary lifestyle) are living miles apart. Today, my body is heavy. My muscles are tight, and my joints sometimes ache but, I know that this isn't true for me. I know that this body is the result of a life lived out of alignment with who I really am.

My true self is strong, healthy, and vibrant.

I want my reality and my truth to be the same. I believe we all do. After spending all of this time fighting to move the mountain that lives in the gap between the two, suddenly I see how the old way of thinking has failed me. The old way is not working. In fact, it never works. We have to find a way to get back into alignment with our truth.

If your mountain is finances, you might be learning to create and live according to a budget, establishing a savings plan, furthering your education or pursuing a passion in your spare time (in order to cultivate extra income). If your mountain is relationships, you might make more phone calls, write more letters, play more games, plan more dates, etc. If your mountain is health, we might be looking at some of the same terrain but yours may also look very different.

It may be that drinking hundreds of gallons of water is necessary for you to make your way over this mountain but you only have to drink it one glass at a time. Instead of freaking out and declaring that you've had your last diet soda, a strategy that falls flat every single day, perhaps you can drink a bottle of water before each soda. It would both increase your water intake and slow down the incoming soda.

While I don't drink soda any more, I realized recently that my water intake fallen quite low again. I bought a new water bottle and calculated how many I need to drink a day. There are a dozen ways to encourage myself to to get more water in my body, so I picked one and stuck with it. Also, we joined a gym and have been working out most days each week. Again, there are many ways to encourage ourselves to move the body. Let's find one and commit.

This is about walks in the park and the roar of my blender making smoothies — not once and certainly not all day, every single day of the rest of my life — but again and again and again. This is about me being willing to feel whatever comes up, instead of stuffing my feelings back down with food. It's going to take all of these things… one at a time.

And I've done lots of nothing before, primarily because I couldn't do everything. That's what we do, those of us who see that other path in the distance and want to undo years of wandering in one gigantic shove. We try and fail. We get stuck on the other side of the mountain.

It doesn't have to be this way.

When I tried to climb the mountain, I found out that it takes strength that I don't have to conquer it. (And when you slip, the fall is vicious). I tried to go back to the fork in the road, hoping to undo my missteps but it turns out, those old signs are all grown over now. Going backward never took me anywhere I actually wanted to go.

I've tried to keep moving forward on the not-quite-right path with the hope that eventually it would curve around the base of the mountain and run into my true path. I still slip into that old complacency sometimes but if I'm being honest, it never actually takes me home. It just gives me more time to recognize my suffering. Ironically, that is always the same exact amount of time I need to build strength for the journey home.

Okay, that probably sounds a little hopeless but don't worry. There's one more thing.

Every time you make a promise to take action that brings you closer to yourself — and keep it — your life changes a little bit. Every time you forgive someone else, your life changes a little bit and when you forgive yourself, it changes a great deal. Every time you are gentle with yourself, you get to be more you.

The mountain between reality and truth isn't a mountain at all. It's a pile of pebbles and every single action you take closes the gap a little more — every glass of water, every walk, every moment of kindness and understanding you give yourself. Every single song you dance to, every single piece of art you create, every time you wait to answer until your truth bubbles up.

Obviously this chapter isn't about clutter, it's about life. It's about getting up every day and doing the little things that will cultivate the life you desire, the life that's true for you.

And this book isn't about clutter at all, it's about freedom. So, what is it that you wanted badly enough to release all that you've released? Is it creativity? Love? Health? Is it a professional freedom you desire? Do you have it clear in your mind? Good, now think about all that needs to be done to get you from here to there.

What little pebble can you move today to bring you back to the one you were born to be?

Remember, every single pebble takes you home to you. Suddenly, instead of a promise to move mountains, this feels like a wonderful race.

Challenge

Look around you. What mountain can you see that's standing between you and the life you desire? Remember it's actually just a pile of pebbles. If it's paper, release 27 pieces. If it's unfinished projects, finish one. If it's a couch that sucks you in for hours, put a coffee table on the damned thing to keep your butt off of it. Create a less cozy spot for your computer if you go to check your email and find that time just disappears. If it's a person... well, that's probably beyond the scope of this book but you know what needs to be done, don't you? Find something, your choice, and deal with it. Today.

Gifts
and Other Charismatic Clutter

I always loved my mom's wedding ring and I lovingly harassed her for years about how, since she and my father were divorced, she didn't need it anymore. She'd had the engagement diamond set among the smaller diamonds in the band and had been single forever, so it didn't feel like a wedding ring to me. It was a diamond ring that, like me, had its origin in my parent's relationship but wasn't really about them anymore.

Wow, I don't think I ever realized that about the ring and me until just now when I typed it. That happens a great deal with this process. As we audition the items in our physical space (to see if they are of more value to us than the space they occupy), we sometimes discover surprising details of our relationship with those things.

If we ask the right questions, these things will offer us the deeper, more intimate details. We will discover the secret stories between us and our stuff.

- Where did this item come from?

- What does it mean to me?

- Do I use this item, why or why not?

- How would my life be different without it?

Anyway, for years I offered to take that ring off of her hands, to enjoy it on her behalf, and on my 21st birthday she gave it to me. I was surprised. She told me later that she'd worked hard to convince me that I'd never get it so I would be able to be surprised to receive it.

I was thrilled to have that ring… for a while.

But then there was a time, somewhere beyond all of the harassing and the gift giving when my tastes began to change. Perhaps not change but rather, emerge. I was fresh into adulthood and I started to get to know myself. I found out I'm not a yellow gold kind of woman. I like silver and platinum and before too long, my special family treasure was spending its days and nights in the jewelry box tucked safely away in my closet.

I had options. I considered having the diamonds reset into something that I'd enjoy wearing. I considered just letting it sit there in my jewelry box. I didn't consider selling it but I could have. I could have put it away for my own daughter, which would have been some sort of crazy extended re-gifting timeline because when this went down, she wasn't yet born.

As I considered my options, ironically, my mom kept popping up. She loved that ring. She'd only parted with it because she loved me too. In the end, I gave it back to her. I asked her to wear it for me for a while.

That's the thing about gifts. We give them in love because it feels like a good idea. We can't possibly know if it actually is the perfect gift, that the recipient will love it and use it. We can't know if they want this exact thing, in this color, shape, and size, and there is no way in the world we can assume that it will be perfect for them forever. We don't give to harness people with the stuff we thought was a good idea.

This is the same for the gifts you receive. If it doesn't serve you, let it go.

Challenge

Find every single gift that you've received that you don't absolutely LOVE. Every one. Yes, all of them. And that one too. I understand that your friend was very excited. I realize that your aunt meant well. I can see how you might be worried about your mom being mad. She may very well be mad but, I'm not scared. Tell her to call me. I can explain it. This stuff has you stuck and it has to go!

Causes of Clutter:
Food Edition

I met sweetness on the first day of my life, sugar water in the hospital nursery while my mother recovered from the childbirth by surgery. I imagine that everyone I encountered on that first day would be shocked to know how much of the 40 years that followed would be occupied by my relationship with sugar.

Little of the next decade is available to me but I do have a string of candy-laced memories, strangely clear recollections of celebrations and everyday life filled with both homemade goodness and pre-packaged treats. In hindsight, I can see that all of this was grooming me for what would eventually become a life-altering addictive relationship with food.

I was in the sixth grade when this simple, rather common exposure to sweetness blossomed into something more like an adulterous affair. Complete with secrets, betrayal, irresistible attraction, and lapses in integrity that were subtle — almost harmless — in the beginning but intensified as the grips of this thing had its way with me. At first, it was an act of desperation. Perhaps that's where all addictive relationships begin.

Desperate for control of anything in my life and longing for some appropriate measure of autonomy for a 12-year old, I wanted to feel... whole, something that remained unnamed for many, many more years. The shift into the darkness of my fall from truth was almost undetectable. One morning, I slipped a few quarters out of my dad's change jar for an after school "treat" — a coke and a candy bar from the Circle K that I walked past on my way home from school each afternoon.

I felt liberated, having just that little bit of money at my disposal, being able to choose how to invest it in the betterment of my day. I could have done anything with it — a fancy, new pen and notebook from the school bookstore or an extra dessert at lunch. Again, it was about having power, control of something, anything in my life and certainly comfort too. Food intake wasn't monitored at home but it was noticed. Everything was noticed.

Little was tolerated, even things that in hindsight I can see are normal kid behaviors.

One night a couple of girls slept over and in the wee hours of the night we crept into the kitchen for party food, which included a jar of pickle spears that we emptied. I remember feeling like I would be in trouble, or probably worse yet, perceived as a foolish and out-of-control girl with equally irresponsible friends.

My perceptions of these stories are absolutely impossible to separate from the reality, as they have become one. The truth officially eclipsed by my truth, or perhaps a collection of my truths are all the truth that ever exists. I can't tell any more, leaving me certain of only one thing: None of this matters to the little girl inside of me. She felt ashamed. I felt ashamed to be me.

Buying the after-school treats with my dad's change made me feel big, and my friends were impressed I was "allowed" to do that. They seemed to enjoy it when my impulse to treat spread to them. Yes, before I was even out of middle school, I'd decided that sharing my love of sweetness with others made them like me more. Clearly, that's a dangerous belief no matter what kind of treats I was going to use to buy my friends.

All of this worked for me, not the long run of course, but in the beginning. These coping mechanisms always work in the beginning. That's how they get their hooks in us. It worked because I could consume the sugary goodness and dispose of the evidence — the soda can added to the recycling bin and candy wrapper buried deep within the trash can at home — leaving nothing for anyone who might disapprove to notice.

It was an act of misguided self-love, a desperate attempt to meet unmet needs but the reality is that when I was still a child, I started trying to fill the big, black hole in my soul with sweets. And also I used dysfunctional relationships.

In hindsight, I can see that they were fairly effective tools for a young, already very broken-hearted girl who needed desperately to feel better. I felt treated, a sense of luxury in a world where it otherwise didn't exist, and cool, or whatever that thing is that drives one to sacrifice their sanity to secure a social position, or at least attempt to secure a social position.

Fast-forward twenty-five years and you have me, today. When I'm afraid, I want sweets. When I'm lonely, I want sweets. When I'm sad or overwhelmed or sleepy, I want sweets. When I want someone to know I love them, my impulse is to shower them with sweets. When I am angry, and even when I want to celebrate, my heart aches for my old friend. My mind searches desperately for that which it knows worked beautifully in the past. It's not even a desire. It's a need.

I haven't had a soda in more than ten years now, and it's been four days since I ate cake. These affairs we have — the relationships that begin and grow from a wounded place, as opposed to a place of love, feel impossible to walk away from. They have their claws hooked firmly into us, and we are profoundly dependent on them in return. It's a black hole and once we're hooked, the relationship hurls us deeper into the need, leaving us more and more weak to resist.

This is my story, a sliver of it really, but I once found myself sharing all of this on a group call for one my space healing workshops. Every day, I issue a challenge to move them forward in the quest for simplicity and on that day it was to release any food clutter, those items in our fridges, freezers, pantries, and cabinets, that no longer serve us.

It turns out, for many, this task threatened something very deep within. We spoke of old hauntings about not having enough food. For some those fears were born of a previous generation's depression-altered reality, and for others it was their own hungry childhoods that gave birth to these beliefs. All driven by different stories, we are all using food to try to make ourselves feel better.

Every person on that call accepted the invitation to look back, to explore the foundations of their fears and beliefs about food, the very messages that lead us to buy more than we need, will use, or can afford. We noticed that sometimes when we are feeling insecure about our keeping a roof over our heads, we fill up our pantries out of desperation. It is an understandable desperation to feel secure, one that falls short of actually providing the kinds of security we need and desire.

We took the hour to explore our stories, to share them, and it continues to blow my mind how much freedom is found in the sharing of our secrets. I've always suspected that it wasn't actually the weight of the stuff or the power of our addiction that most keeps us stuck but rather our shame that traps us in these patterns.

Addiction. Secrets. Lies. It always comes back to the shame but if we can find the courage to whisper our truth — if only to ourselves at first and eventually to others who will honor us with non-judgment — we can break free of the past, of our pain, and of that which paralyzes us and keeps us feeling stuck.

Challenge

Clear your food clutter! Remember your fridge, freezer, pantry, and cabinets, etc. Even the candy dish or wherever else you stash food. Check the expiration dates. Check the quality. Are you going to eat this? Is this going to serve you when you do? Why haven't you eaten this, yet? What would need to happen for you to prepare and eat this? Do that or let it go.

Consider donating "donate-able" items to a local food pantry, or share with people in your circle (using Facebook or whatever you use) that you've got food that no longer serves to see if anyone else might be able to use it. (For example, my neighbor who just went gluten-free sent a few snacky things down the way to houses with kids who eat those snacky foods.)

Crafting Your Personal Space Healing Strategy

I had a midwife years ago who described an adult-hood worth of hilarious attempts to outrun mid-wifery. She'd get fed up and wash her hands of the whole childbirth thing, pack up her family, and move to a new place where nobody knew her name. Of course, one thing would lead to the next and inevitably she'd stumble upon a birthing woman in the produce department at the grocery store. This story was dramatized for effect but I'm sure you catch my drift, her calling just kept calling.

I feel that way about people and their stuff. First, as a professional organizer and now sharing these methods as I have for the last four years, I just keep coming back to these same ideas.

Everything seemed to be going brilliantly until I noticed that, at least for some people, the intensity of this process had begun to fade. The swell of excitement was receding and their direction felt murky again. They were unclear about what to do, and uninspired to do much of what they could see needed to be done. A couple of them, some who'd already cultivated rather remarkable success, began to wander off. I feared they were losing sight of the end game.

It turns out, I forgot to mention the end game.

(Enter the separation of backlog and maintenance.)

Working with me — whether as a professional organizer in the past, or as I come to you now — is not a forever deal. What you gain during our time together, you certainly get to keep but it is going to be because you've changed, not because I'm sticking around to feed you the same tasty dish again and again.

I get in, stay as long as I need to stay to get the job done, and get out. That's how I roll.

We may work together again when new challenges arise but I'm the one you want on board when life catches fire. I'm not an everyday, carry-on-for-years-and-years kind of support person. So, people hire me because they are sick of being stuck and agree to give my ideas a try for the sole purpose of getting things moving in their worlds again. As metaphors go, think a river blocked by trees and rocks and whatever else that were rearranged in the recent storm.

My job has two parts: 1) to support you through the process of getting unstuck and 2) to support you in establishing new habits that cultivate continued flow.

Perhaps you've met the latter before? It's maintenance, and that which has not been well maintained is your backlog. If maintenance is all the stuff we do on a daily, weekly, monthly, and annual basis to keep things from getting out of hand, the backlog is what piles up when we don't do maintenance.

If we are talking about weight, maintenance is the management of calories in and out. In personal finance maintenance is the management of dollars in and out. Since the whole space healing experience is about getting things moving in our physical space, maintenance is the management of stuff that flows in and out of our possession.

If you were already in maintenance mode, then you'd already be doing what needs to be done and you probably wouldn't have read all of the way through this book.

But if you have a backlog, it is my hope that the information and inspiration offered on these pages will help you eliminate the backlog and get on track with a solid maintenance plan. But mind games and stories are not enough. You need a plan. I want to help you create one to support you as you transition to working on your own. Again, it's not fancy. I don't believe it needs to be. It just needs to be true for you and it needs to help you to move past thinking about all of this stuff and into taking action.

Space healing is about taking back your space, systematically and with great determination — to eliminate the backlog, which will leave you with a maintenance system for your physical environment.

Here are eight elements your personal space healing strategy needs to include.

Vision

It starts with vision. This is the dream, the goal, the blueprint of what you want your space to feel like and how you want it to support you. If you were making a change in your physical body, then it might be a clothing size or measurements or weight or even an activity-based goal like running a 5K race. Since we are talking about space, this is what you want it to look like when the backlog is completely gone. It doesn't mean you'll never clean or release excess again, it just means you do it when it's time instead of letting it build up.

Crafting a vision can be tricky for some people. If you don't have a clear vision, take some time to explore what's possible and choose a style that captures the way you want your home to feel. This might mean picking a word that resonates for you (temple, sanctuary, studio, nest, home, locker room, cottage, etc.). Or think about places that you've been that feel like you want your home to feel. Once you find a vision, really lean into it. Move toward it by holding it in your mind while you audition your backlog. "Is this item consistent with my vision for this space?"

Reality

This is the "get real with yourself" portion of any successful backlog elimination strategy. Get your head out of the sand and look at where you are after reading this book. Look around, take more pictures, accept that this is your next launching point. Whether you've done the challenges or not, it's time to commit to whatever it takes to heal your space. Let go of the judgement and shame and just be with what is.

Gap

Mind the gap, as they say. Notice the distance between your vision and your reality. What's it going to take to close that gap? Measure it, if that's possible. If you're working on clutter, walk around in your space and ask your brain to recognize which items are standing between your reality and your vision. All of that has to go.

Time

By what date do you want the gap closed? It might be a week or a year or even more, depending on the goal and the amount of time you have each day or week or month to give to this process.

Action

Given the gap and the time frame you've chosen, what do you need to do to make it happen? Start by committing to a small, daily action that is within your means... and then do it. It could be 15 minutes a day or an hour, or eight hours. If you can't make a commitment to daily action, pick a larger chunk of time once a week, or one full day or weekend each month. Choose whatever it's going to take to get done what must be done in the amount of time you can tolerate working on the backlog phase of this process.

Making promises to ourselves and keeping them, even tiny ones, will build energy and space in your life to accommodate this change.

Flexibility

You're human. Get over it. You will face obstacles. Don't give up, deal with them. And while you're figuring out all of that, be gentle with yourself. If beating ourselves up had ever helped anyone, I'd at least be willing to consider it as a strategy but it hasn't. So, stop being violent with yourself. If you can't, get help.

Accountability

Make your commitment and then do it. If your commitment was to walk 30 minutes a day, and you realized that you were too tired to walk at the end of the day on Tuesdays because you have class after a full day of work, then I'd tell you to get up 30 minutes early on Tuesdays or walk on your lunch break or during your kid's soccer practice. Working on your space is the same. You may have to get crafty to do it but keep your promises to yourself… no matter what.

Now, if you broke a leg and it was suddenly not possible for you to keep your promise, then adjust your commitment to something different, something doable, that in some way keeps you moving toward your vision. Get a friend to come help out. Add more time to your plan. Whatever it takes, adjust. Don't run away.

Support

Do these steps and then take the action. If you get stuck, take whatever action is necessary to get you moving forward again. That's all it takes to make a change, just keep moving forward.

If the challenge is too emotionally intense, adjust it and commit to an action that you can actually take each day. If daily challenges are impossible because of your other commitments, then do one each week. If you're sick, go to bed. Just remember that in bed you're probably not moving forward, so don't stay there any longer than you need to!

If you know that this journey is true for you — if there's a backlog in your physical space and it's impacting the rest of your life — and if you're tired of putting up with it but you feel paralyzed, take control of your life by getting the support you need. If reading this book is enough, awesome! If you need more support, take a workshop or recruit support from your local community. Get what you need because there isn't anyone else who's agreed to be in charge of that part.

Whatever it is, just do what needs to be done. And once it's done, once the backlog is eliminated, close this chapter of the journey. You're just maintaining your physical space now. The deficit is gone. The baggage has been released. It's okay to move on.

This is not Hotel California, and as far as I'm concerned, you are not staying here.

Your Final Challenge

Grab a piece of paper. This one is a writing assignment. And it's an important one, so give me a few minutes to help you transition to your own Personal Space Healing Strategy.

First, write a list of every single space in your home. Add to that list any other places where you have stuff (mom's attic, storage units, work, even the car if it is chaotic).

Now, pick a place to start. One room, or if that's too much, pick one zone inside one room. If you can't face The Kitchen, break it down into zones — countertop, pantry, upper cabinets, lower cabinets, under the sink, etc. If even that's too much to face, number those cabinets (cabinet #1, #2, ...). You are going to make each space as small as you need to make it to be willing to face it. This works for all spaces, although the zones in a living room might be pile #1, pile #2, bookcase, coffee table, etc.

Now, don't get worked up about which room goes first. It doesn't matter. Some people want to pick the highest point in their house and flow like a waterfall from room to room. Other people start with the smallest space or the space that will be easiest to finish and go from there.

Once you have a room in maintenance mode, maintain it. Don't go in and start a new backlog. Keep up what's happening behind you as you move into the new spaces.

This will give you a methodical way to move through the work that lies ahead. Pick a space and work on it with your daily action, applying all of the new ideas that you've found inside this book (and anywhere else you find them). If you can't finish a whole room in one session, just stop and come back to that same activity the next day. This will keep you from getting stuck in the mental merry-go-round.

How Much Stuff Is Too Much Stuff?

The allergy season has me seeing clutter a little more clearly. This morning, through my red and swollen eyes, the thin layer of dust and pollen which has settled over the interior of my home became my enemy. It's a more subtle version of the layer that's settled over my city. The vehicles, windows, and lawn furniture are all sporting that ominous yellow top coat of death. It's one thing to deal with sensitivities to cats and dust, but, add pollen and I feel like I'm being assaulted.

This is that season every year when I want to slip away to live in a small concrete room with no furnishings. Once a day, I would use a hose and one of those hearty industrial brooms to wash away all of the allergens. I would take with me only what fit in a backpack, which I would pack and sit just outside the door while I cleaned. I think the whole process would take about five minutes and on days like today, it sounds absolutely dreamy.

Instead, I live here, in the real world, where turning a hose on the place would do far more harm than good and so, sadly, I must dust.

This is one of the roots of my resistance to keeping anything that no longer serves me. I don't want anything else to maintain. I don't want to spend the extra time and energy dusting vases, bowls, trinkets, and whatever other assorted whatnot unless I absolutely love them or use them often. I don't want to get on my hands and knees to scrub more bathtubs than we need to function as a family. I don't want to lose precious energy sorting and filing papers that I don't actually need to keep.

I don't want to spend hours and hours of my life tending my stuff. I want to live my life. And even worse, most of us who have stuff that no longer serves us aren't actually spending the hours that it takes each month to properly maintain all of the stuff in our space. So, our garages are full of stuff that we don't use and it's eventually covered with layers of dust and spider webs and whatever else blows in when the doors are open.

If it's too much to dust, isn't it too much to keep? Seriously, if we don't have it in us to keep all of this stuff clean, are we not living beyond our means?

Our bathroom cabinets are filled with stuff we haven't used in years. It's dusty and grimy but we don't pause every week or so to maintain it. Instead we stop opening the drawers and leave the new version of that same stuff on the counter so we can see it. We don't take time to dust and straighten our piles of paper, so the mountain shifts and grows and soon gains landslide potential.

So, what if we could shift the way we see our space? What if, instead of thinking that all this stuff is so vital, we considered the space our most precious commodity? What if we auditioned the things in our home to see if they are of enough value to us to justify the resources — time, money, energy, etc. — that it takes to maintain them?

What if we decided that living was more important than having? And what if that simple decision could free us to have more of what we really long for in our lives? Every single day someone tells me about how they wish they had the time/money/space/energy to read, learn, create, play, love, exercise, eat healthy, make money, travel, etc. Aren't those desires valid too?

Why would we allow this stuff to keep us from loving our lives? Is it really more important just because it made it through the front door already? We can't fall for that! "This stuff was here first" is a terrible reason to not be healthy or love well or create or heal. We all deserve better than this.

Take a deep breath and repeat after me: If it's too much to maintain, it's too much.

Release Responsibly

Clutter clearing is a powerful way to free yourself from that which has you stuck. Before we go any further, we need to talk about what to do with the stuff once you are ready to let it go.

Basically, it comes down to this: Release as responsibly as you can bear to.

When you are paralyzed, the most important thing is that you release the stuff that no longer serves you. This will get the energy moving again. Every single item you release, puts you a bit more back in control of your life. Selling the idea that releasing clutter will give you back your life isn't the purpose of this part of the book but if I haven't already convinced you, just try it. It works. It works better than everything else I've done, regardless of what I was changing, and my community is finding the same.

There are only three reasons we have more stuff than space. It's important that you address all three reasons.

1. We bring in (or allow in) more stuff than our space can hold.

2. We don't feel inclined or able to release the excess in our space.

3. We don't know how to get the excess out of our space.

For some people, those who are dreadfully stuck, all they can summon the strength to do is put the excess in a trash bag and haul it out to the curb. If that's all you can do, do it. Do whatever you can to get started, even asking for help if necessary. As soon as you can do better (than sending everything to the landfill), do better.

For everyone who isn't that completely paralyzed, do better now. So, what is "better" when it comes to clutter clearing? Basically, everything between keeping it in your house and you putting it in the landfill is better in my book. The more care you take to put your stuff in the best possible place, the more earth-friendly your healing journey will be.

We all know there are lots of options when it comes to bringing stuff into our homes. It's important that we remember that there are also lots of options for sending it out. Some communities have one parking lot with trash drop off, recycling bins, and an organization collecting donated goods. Even if they aren't all centrally located like that, these basic options are available almost everywhere and if you donate everything you can and then recycle all you can of what remains, what ends up in the landfill will be minimal. This is the easiest, most straight-forward, almost-everyone-can-do-this approach to releasing respectfully.

There are other organizations which offer easy drop off locations and some will even pick up. I could list a bunch of them here but then you might miss out of other extraordinary organizations in your community. Do a little leg work. Find out what the needs are in your community and do your part to meet them. Just Google "donate [insert your city]" and you'll find lots of options.

If you have a specific item you want to find a better home for, Google that too. For example, "donate women business clothes [your city]" (adjusting, of course, for your item) returns results for local organizations that will be deliriously happy to get the stuff you no longer use into the hands of those that need them.

Google "donate food (your city)" and unload some of the excess in your kitchen before it spoils. People all over this country are literally starving. When you release that which no longer serves you, it supports others in ways you may not be able to imagine.

I've had some of the coolest one family to another clutter clearing experiences, both when people gave my family things that we needed and when we've given things we no longer needed to other families. Whether it's clothing that children have outgrown, extra office supplies, or recently upgraded electronics, when I do the extra work of finding someone who needs that exact thing... there simply is not a better feeling. I'm free of that thing and the other person's need is filled, or the other way around.

There are many ways to find people who have a need for the thing you are ready to release. I've used Craigslist, Freecycle, and even a Facebook group set up for buying, selling, and giving away items in my community. I've asked friends if they needed items or if they knew anyone else who might. I've contacted churches. I've reached out to domestic violence shelters and animal shelters. They both have many specific needs and I promise that your generosity will change lives.

If you have items with historical relevance — for your family, community, or otherwise — find someone else who wants to archive them. You don't have to be the keeper of all of the things that ever landed in your space. Try museums, schools, libraries, theaters, and anyone else who might be able to put your old stuff to use.

If you have toxic items — old paint, cleaning supplies, pesticides, etc. — or appliances or electronics, consider the best outlet for them. If they are functional, take the time to find a place or person that needs them and donate them. If they are broken, you may still be able to donate them but otherwise, dispose of them responsibly. Contact the waste management department in your community. Every place I've lived for the last 20 years has had a website that told me exactly where and when to drop off assorted materials for safe disposal of toxic goods.

Lastly, because it always comes up, let's talk about the money. Once we identify stuff we are ready to release and we've figured out a better way to release it, we're too often afraid to go through with it. We are afraid we won't have enough money to replace it, or that somebody else will have our stuff and we still won't have what we really need and desire. We are afraid, and that's fair, but it isn't going to help. If you can sell it, do it. Get your money and move on. If you can't sell it, on your own or with help, donate it and get the tax write off, or give it away and trust that the space you made will allow what you need to rush in.

Releasing that which no longer serves you from your physical environment will change your life. Period. So, let it go. Stop trying to manage all of this stuff and start living your life. And for those of us who claim to care about one another and the planet, can we afford to cling to stuff that no longer serves us? Are we willing to hoard resources that other people need, when we're not using them?

When that stuff has served its purpose in your life, I'm asking you to release it responsibly. For many of us, this requires redefining waste. And depending how environmentally conscientious you are at this moment, it might be a bit of a transformation.

For the most part, I'm a live-and-let-live kind of girl, but a few years ago there was something going on in my community that really turned my stomach. Writing about it kept me from chaining myself to the dumpster down the street. Dramatic? Yes, but I had to do something.

Week after week, I drove the two-mile stretch between my house and the lot behind the community rec center where those without curbside pickup dropped off trash. We could recycle cardboard, paper, plastic, glass, aluminum and tin, and there was a non-profit organization with a trailer there where we could drop off donations. There were four huge bins for assorted types of waste destined for the landfill.

In that small town, it could not be any easier to let go of that which no longer serves us in a way that honors the earth. And still, every week, when I arrived with my car full of stuff we were done with, I'd pull in behind someone hurling a truck full of recyclable and donate-able goods straight into the landfill-bound bins.

After four years of this same experience over and over again, I felt ready to come undone. Why aren't we all doing everything in our power to keep all but true waste out of the landfill?

I confessed to the guy who runs that whole operation that I found it so upsetting. He said it happens all day, every day, and that he hates that he can't do anything about it. He can't force people to drive the extra 30 feet to drop their cardboard into the recycling bins. (And sometimes it is already broken down.) He can't ask them to donate that perfectly good sink to a local non-profit organization. He can't refuse them, and frankly, I'm not sure that chaining myself to trash bins would have cultivated much more than traffic and frustration.

What will it take for this situation to change? Quite simply, we have to redefine waste.

In my clutter clearing classes, I ask my students to release as responsibly as possible. The truth is, I want my neighbors to do the same. I want the landfill to be reserved for those things that we haven't yet figured out how to reuse and recycle because that is the essence of true waste.

The rest of it can be reused or recycled, and putting it in the landfill is a waste of money, land, and precious resources that can never again be utilized by its owner or anyone else. By depositing non-waste in the landfill we prematurely remove it from the general flow of stuff in our society. It's like sending people to the cemetery before they are dead. In many cases, long before they are dead!

Books can be read again and again, and when people are no longer willing to read them, they can be recycled. People who get fancy new electronics, clothes, and kitchenware (and everything else we purchase) can release their old ones back into the general flow of stuff (that runs through neighborhoods and communities throughout the land) by selling them, giving them away, or donating them to an organization that resells at a low price or distributes them to people who cannot otherwise afford to purchase new. If we acquire new towels, we turn our old towels into cleaning towels, or if they are still in great shape, we can ask around to see if anyone can use a linen upgrade. Also, animal shelters and rehab groups everywhere are eager to receive our old towels.

When we are ready to release an item that no longer serves us, we can't assume that means it's ready for the landfill. Living more sustainably demands that we redefine waste.

So, what if I ask you nicely? Yes, I'm proposing a shift in our collective definition of waste, or that which ends up in the landfill.

I'm not the first. This is not a new idea. In fact, I've been living this way for years. (In part, thanks to my grandparents who were recycling paper and cans twenty-five years ago.) My family produces one bag of landfill-bound trash about every six days. We reuse what we can, find good homes for the stuff we're done with, and recycle what can be recycled. The rest is, for my family, true waste. We are not, by any stretch of the imagination, living some environmentally extreme existence. It's just that easy to release responsibly once you shift your thinking about what landfills are for.

So, here I am asking for an (admittedly unlikely) shift in the way the collective 'we' defines waste. I'm even asking nicely, like I learned in preschool. Can we, pretty please with sugar on top, redefine waste and shift our habits accordingly?

What if asking nicely isn't enough?

While trying to sort out my thoughts on waste, I felt compelled to talk to someone who knows more about these matters than I do. I asked around, scored the jackpot of referrals, and ended up talking to a terribly cool dude named Johnny Shields. He and his wife Tara owned The Green Wagon East Nashville and he is a graduate of the Institute for Sustainable Practice at Lipscomb University. After introductions, our conversation started something like this (loosely paraphrased for your amusement):

> *Me:* I'm proposing a shift in the way we define waste. Ultimately, that's what we want, right?
>
> *Cool dude:* Yes.
>
> *Me:* Can we do it?
>
> (Pause)
>
> *Cool dude:* No.

Because I knew the odds were stacked against me, I wasn't crushed by his reality check. He doesn't believe it is likely that the collective we will make the shift. Certainly, we can but we probably won't. When I asked what it would take, some of what I learned suggests that we might want to make a change because I asked nicely.

1. It won't need to be "more convenient" as in curbside recycling pick up for everyone. It

will need to be "more convenient" as in free to recycle and compost and, therefore, more expensive to send stuff to the landfill. That's right, people will be inspired to act more thoughtfully when it becomes a financial hardship to dispose of trash.

2. If consumers have to pay more for waste, they will start making more packaging-conscious purchases. This will create pressure for manufacturers to package with more environmental awareness.

3. The "freedom" mentality is hurting the environment. We, at least in the United States, have this misplaced arrogance about being free to do whatever the heck we want. That's not real. We aren't free to do harm to others, and living so incredibly wastefully is toxic to the land, water, air, and people who share this planet with us.

Side note: I've always wondered where people think "away" is when they are throwing stuff away. There is no away, it's a hole in the ground right down the road from all of us and the stuff we send there takes shocking numbers of years to decompose (like 600 years for fishing line).

Here is the summary of my reality check (and ironically the only thing that may make me asking nicely sound like a good idea):

This is changing. It's not changing fast enough. We are doing harm to the planet and the people who live on it. We are better than this. If we don't do better, the government is going to force us to.

I'll be honest. I didn't think it would come down to this when I started exploring this topic, but look around. There is evidence everywhere that what I'm proposing is true. We are consumers, and the manufacturers bow at our knees. We are the decision makers, and it's up to us to decide where our stuff goes when we are done with it. We have the power to make a difference, right now, by putting those cardboard boxes in the recycling bins instead of sending them to the landfill.

Wouldn't it be amazing if we could, just this once, fix something we screwed up before the government forced us to?

Unstuck

It's been four years since I started writing this book. All that remains is to conclude it. Tonight, as I put pen to paper, my mind is occupied by the endless line of brave souls whose stories got me out of bed every morning.

There's the woman whose home and life had been frozen in the winter of her husband's long, heartbreaking battle with cancer. Everything had been on hold for years before she came into my life and little by little, one day at a time, she started to take back her life. There were lots of energetic blocks to move through, many tears were shed along the way. But there were healing stories, breathtaking breakthroughs, and lots of laughter, too.

And that's just one woman. She lived eight time zones away from me. Closer to home, there was the woman whose space healing journey helped her close the door on a marriage to a man who'd been betraying her since before their wedding. There was another who'd moved so many times that she'd quit unpacking and hanging pictures on the wall. She couldn't bear to settle again but she came to me miserable because she wouldn't allow herself to make home. There was an artist whose home didn't inspire, her studio so overrun with ideas that new ideas couldn't bubble up, let alone come to life.

From my vantage point tonight, I can see so clearly how this space healing journey really isn't about clutter. I mean, of course it's about clutter. It's all about how our external space mirrors what lives within us. Space healing heals our hearts.

This work can potentially be deeply transformative. I think that's why it's felt so hard to finish writing the book. There are so many stories, ideas, and mind games that I want to share with you. Believe it or not, I'm already haunted by all that fell outside the scope of this project — engaging resistant partners, releasing mental clutter, and sharing space healing with children you raised with your old ways of being. That handful of seeds are collected in a file, awaiting their turn, with the intention that what's next will come through in a fraction of the time it took the first.

And that's not just a pipe dream, you know? Space healing makes it possible to bring our dreams to life.

It took me four years to become the woman who is capable of writing the book you are holding in your hands. And I never have to go back to being the woman I was before all of this started. This personal evolution is mine and the woman I have become is the one I will be at the beginning of this next project. I am changed. What I'm capable of creating has changed with me.

The clarity that comes from this journey allows us to be more productive, sane, creative, healthy, abundant, bold, powerful, and every single other thing we know lives within us but that we haven't been able to access because of old heartbreak. It allows us to feel more alive. To release what no longer serves us and make space for what's true brings us into alignment with our true selves. It's empowering. Give yourself this gift because the world isn't just waiting for me to write this book.

We need you to do what you came here to do.

Made in the USA
Las Vegas, NV
16 April 2021